LEYLAND HERITAGE

LEYLAND HERITAGE

Alan Thomas

Published in association
with the British Motor
Industry Heritage Trust

TEMPLE PRESS

Frontispiece: A Thornycroft of the late
1940s at St Pauls. Thornycroft was one
of several builders of premium quality
vehicles which, after a long history of
independence, found that it no longer
possessed sufficient design and
production capacity to maintain a
commercially attractive market share.
Like others before and after, the
company threw in its lot with a bigger
and stronger group – which in the
fullness of time joined what is now
British Leyland.

The publishers are grateful to the
following individuals and
organisations for the illustrations in
this book: John Aldridge; Piers
Cavendish/Louise Olivier; Bill
Godwin; The Leyland Group; *Motor
Transport*; Ian Muggeridge; Tony
Porter and Alan Thomas.

Published by Temple Press
an imprint of Newnes Books
84/88 The Centre, Feltham, Middlesex, TW13 4BH, England
and distributed for them by
The Hamlyn Publishing Group Limited
Rushden, Northants, England

ISBN 0 600 35063 0
Printed in Spain

Contents

Falling into disaster

To a degree unrivalled anywhere else in industry those divisions of British Leyland which made, and make, commercial vehicles have been bedevilled by their own history. The roots of BL as a whole are long established and run deeply: many of the constituent companies traced their origins back into the 1880s and even earlier, and most once reflected the dominant personalities of the men who made and guided them.

Inevitably, as the years went by, these often small businesses changed their natures, coalesced, faded. Such organic processes, matching similar patterns of growth and development among vehicle users, followed what can be seen with hindsight as a relatively orderly pattern: for a year or two after a merger existing products would continue, until superseded by unified ranges; spares and service backup lasted a few years more; within a decade virtually all trace of a once-famous 'partner' would have gone.

However, as the process of amalgamation accelerated during the 1960s, and except in the narrowest legal sense, events within British Leyland became anything but orderly. The causes of disorganisation were complicated and often mutually contradictory: even with the benefit of hindsight it is hard to see how the process could have been made more dignified or commercially advantageous. Certainly it became a story of the kind to give nightmares to any business executive – and it is one to fascinate anybody who is in the least interested in road transport and industrial history.

In large part these untoward events came about through the merging of what were essentially mass-production car factories with commercial vehicle makers whose methods still employed a great deal of skilled hand work. But that is too simple an explanation. Perhaps, if the prosperities of the 1950s and 1960s had not existed, it would have been possible to successfully merge staffs, factories, and products. As it was, every vehicle that could be made had a buyer eagerly waiting; in such circumstances it would have been a brave or foolish management that delayed and distracted its production people for the sake of doctrinaire amalgamation. In any case, nearly all the models being made were then quite young: to arbitrarily discontinue any of them would have caused considerable losses through the scrapping of production tools and equipment that had not yet paid for themselves – quite apart from the disruptions of supply inevitable in any product change.

Then there was considerable political interference, which has formed a dark background to post-1939 vehicle manufacture in Britain. There was an inevitability about the well publicised way in which government was ultimately forced to inject huge sums of money into what had become the last British motor manufacturer of any size; less clearly remembered is the overwhelming pressure from politicians of the day which forced the last great merger, that of the Leyland Motor Corporation and British Motor Holdings. And no one can tell how much money was absorbed and effort vitiated over preceding years by government 'encouragement' to establish new factories in so-called development areas, which almost by definition were well away from traditional motor manufacturing districts and suppliers.

During the post-war years most factories were

Opposite centre: The Terrier, a Bathgate-built lightweight in the BMC tradition although introduced by BLMC, was a successful and steady seller for years. Indeed, it became the last of its generation of models in production. The vast majority were goods chassis, but some half-hearted efforts were made to promote it as a small bus – again, the lack of development capital can be discerned. Apart from specimens – some with a set-back front axle which made room for a front entrance – bodied for home market use, a number were sold in France. Stoelen, the Belgian coach-builder, made this and several others for customers in mainland Europe. The EA, another Bathgate goods chassis, was also turned to passenger use.

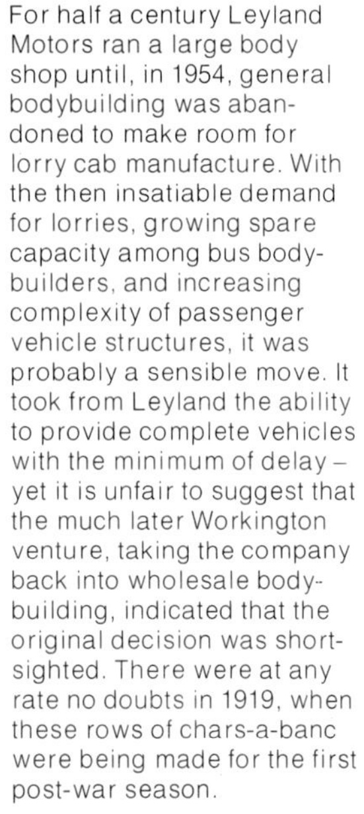

For half a century Leyland Motors ran a large body shop until, in 1954, general bodybuilding was abandoned to make room for lorry cab manufacture. With the then insatiable demand for lorries, growing spare capacity among bus bodybuilders, and increasing complexity of passenger vehicle structures, it was probably a sensible move. It took from Leyland the ability to provide complete vehicles with the minimum of delay – yet it is unfair to suggest that the much later Workington venture, taking the company back into wholesale bodybuilding, indicated that the original decision was shortsighted. There were at any rate no doubts in 1919, when these rows of chars-a-banc were being made for the first post-war season.

An awkward legacy from BMC to BLMC was the absence of any light commercial able to compete on level terms with American-origin vehicles. Traditionally Morris and Austin between them had dominated the market, but by the mid-1960s it was quickly slipping away. Other problems had priority, and it was not until 1975 that a new light van and pick up, Sherpa, could be introduced.

'New' was a relative term, for Sherpa vans evidently owed a great deal to two forebears, the 22 cwt 250JU (**above left**) and the 12 cwt J4. Although a worthy machine the newcomer (**above**) lacked the appeal of its rivals and by the end of the 1970s its demise seemed likely; then the new company improved vehicle reliability and sales efforts – with considerable success.

becoming obsolete, typically comprising widespread ranges of buildings which consisted of extensions, and extensions to extensions, and yet more extensions. In these piecemeal properties, on equally motley production equipment, it was possible to build and regularly revise the simpler vehicles of yesteryear. By the 1960s it became clearer by the month that those firms likeliest to survive as distinct entities were the ones which could break away from the old patterns and to all intents and purposes start afresh, with entirely new products, built on new (and very expensive) machinery, in new factories. Unfortunately government pressures to make such developments away from the motor manufacturing heartlands spoiled many of these enterprises – not all of them Leyland, or destined to become Leyland, companies by any means – before they could succeed.

There were other external influences, more difficult still to combat. For virtually all of its life the British motor industry had held sizeable markets in the British Empire and Commonwealth, and also the many other countries world-

Beginning – more or less – with the First World War subvention designs, Leyland Motors during the 1920s built up a worthwhile trade in Canada. Of course, sentimental ties with the 'Old Country' helped, considerably aided by favourable British Empire trade terms, but Leylands would not have sold for use in that pioneering country if they had not been sturdy and good value. Inevitably, increasing similarity of operating conditions with those in the United States led to American makers gradually dominating the market, and the outbreak of war in 1939 stopped most British exports. Leyland, and others, tried to renew the old contacts after 1945, but it was too late. Another outlet had gone for good.

For most of its years Thorny-croft ranked as one of the top four British commercial vehicle makers, and this 1919 view (**right centre**), of the engine assembly shop gives some indication of the scale of operations even at this early date. Generally the company stayed aloof from merger talk, but serious consideration was given in 1945 to a grouping that would have placed Thornycroft, Leyland, and AEC – with Dennis – under one management. So far as Thornycroft was concerned the failure of this scheme was decisive: by the early 1950s its decline had commenced until finally its huge and underemployed factory at Basingstoke attracted AEC in need of space. It soon became an embarrassment to its new owners, and British Leyland sold it. The airfield crash tenders (**right**) last reminder of the old Thorny-croft flair, were moved to Scammell.

wide that looked to Britain and its reserve Sterling currency. Then quite quickly during the 1960s, the old national horizons were refocused into a narrowly western European outlook. The regular export markets of a lifetime very rapidly became hardly any market at all, for the countries of Europe had by this time revived their own motor industries and products, and had no need to import vehicles made by anyone else.

On the contrary, they were now well placed to take for themselves not only many of the overseas sales that had once been British almost as of right, but also to invade Britain itself. Again the cause was in part at least political: throughout the years of post-war reconstruction other European nations made their state and international highways into a key factor of economic revival. Vehicle design followed, so that when finally the British road network and vehicle legislation caught up with what was already well established practice elsewhere, those rivals had available lorries of all kinds that were not only suitable, but were also in full production. For home factories to meet these changed circumstances enormous

Above: For four decades semi-trailers formed an important part of the Scammell Lorries business – not surprisingly, since the company had virtually single-handedly brought the articulated lorry to Britain. Usually it was a technical leader too, with novel forms of suspension, chassisless construction, and rapid coupling devices to its credit. But major legislative changes in the 1960s fostered the rapid growth of some powerful competitors and Scammell began to slip, despite such workmanlike products as this platform-cum-coil carrier. BLMC made some half-hearted attempts to reinvigorate the operation, but rapid changes of location and identity were not enough. Ultimately Scammell Trailers was sold to a competitor.

Immediately after British Motor Holdings passed into Leyland control the troubles began – or, more accurately, continued and worsened. Despite a huge and often overlapping range of goods chassis the group had nothing with which to fend off competition from imports, until in 1973 Marathon appeared. It had been developed quickly and at irreducible cost, yet it had the makings of an excellent vehicle. Although a standard power unit was an AEC derivative, Marathon was also intended to offer buyers a choice of proprietary engines, including the Cummins exposed by this tilted cab (**right**). Indeed, the whole was essentially an amalgam of parts already used elsewhere in the group (**below right**). Later versions earned a sound reputation, but were soon outclassed by competitors.

Left: It was no secret that the British Motor Corporation wanted to build its new truck assembly plant within the company's west Midlands heartland. But national governments have wider perspectives, and BMC was induced to make its investment in economically depressed southern Scotland. Bathgate opened in 1961: those models which carried on the light and medium weight traditions of Austin and Morris were reasonably successful; ventures into heavier products less so. The whole added to the problems facing British Leyland management: some common sourcing of components and sub-assemblies followed. Later production of what was left of the erstwhile Albion range was also transferred to Bathgate.

Above: BMC had been among the first makers in Europe to predict a large potential demand for a factory-produced van in the 1·5 to 2 tons capacity range, and accordingly set to work on the model which became the EA. It was intended to inherit the considerable goodwill generated by many years of the LD, a vehicle similar in layout but which needed coachbuilt bodywork. EA was to be all pressed steel. In many ways the production version was ideal, but inadequate testing and development soon gave it a bad name for expensive unreliability. BLMC extensively rethought the details and moved production from Birmingham to Bathgate, but by then the damage had been done.

Above right: Yet another example of model wastage was the Standard Atlas light commercial of 1959, which had the fashionable engine-between-the-seats layout. Under the wing of Leyland, which bought Standard in 1961, the model was developed into an acceptable tonner for van, pick-up, or small bus use, and as such it formed a useful downward extension of the Leyland range – as this Leyland 20 of 1966 shows. But after the BMH merger, light commercial production was inevitably concentrated with the specialist mass-producers. The Atlas then faded, customer choice was narrowed, and what had been a company asset was such no longer.

investments were required; all the importers had to do was to increase output a little. For the one, huge expenditure and borrowings; for the other, a useful increase in profits.

Yet it has to be said that all these reasons, and more, for the decline of heavy vehicle manufacture in Britain are still only part of the story, for much of the blame undoubtedly lay within the companies themselves. One such company, which was large and highly reputable, felt unable any longer to fend off competition from high volume producers, and merged. A second, much smaller but equally respected, was almost the fiefdom of one man: when he passed, so did his firm. Another long established concern had never tried to replace old boardroom blood with young: ultimately it too fell before a more vigorous rival. A fourth, more by accident than design, found it had become too large and diffuse for control by available management. A fifth devoted ever more of its resources to car making and starved the

Once the Land-Rover had established a sound market for its four-wheel-drive vehicles it was not long before Austin too produced one of the same kind. It was named the Champ, and met with some success in military use. There was a civilian version too. By the late 1950s the immediately identifiable Champ had led to the Gipsy, which while mechanically Austin (or BMC) owed a great deal of its looks to the then still competitive Land-Rover. Hopes for the Gipsy were high, as the installation of this assembly line indicates, but it never achieved the success of its rival, and when British Motor Holdings joined Rover-owning Leyland Motor Corporation it was the Gipsy which was abandoned.

commercial vehicle divisions.

All these, and the similar, failings that ultimately led to oblivion might well have responded to vigorous and determined management: in that sense, it was just chance that left Leyland as the final flag carrier. It might have been Thornycroft and could easily have been AEC: perhaps it should have been BMH, for that giant already comprised mass production and specialist car manufacturers, volume and premium commercial vehicle makers, truck and bus model ranges, when it finally fell.

And although ultimate responsibility in such things must lie with senior management, there were plenty of others in less exalted ranks within the companies who also carried large shares of blame. For too long, within many of the earlier merged businesses, efforts devoted at every level to spirited rearguard actions in defence of now-superseded companies and traditions would have been better spent in bringing success to the new

Above While fellow members of the British Leyland group visibly suffered from their collective misfortunes Bristol Commercial Vehicles appeared to sail quiet waters of its own, latterly with a conventional rear-engined double decker, and two single deckers – this one, full-sized and rear-engined, the other a mid-engined lightweight. But inevitably the big single deckers gave way to Leyland Nationals, and the double decker was suppressed in the tidying up which followed the introduction of the present Titan. An attempt was made to keep Bristol in business, but the underworked assembly halls at Workington prevailed: Bristol closed in 1983.

Above and below: When Scammell became a member of the BLMC Construction Equipment division, its road haulage vehicles competed for sales with those of the Truck and Bus division. Originally its Crusader range of the 1970s emphasised double-drive six-wheeled tractors for export and heavy haulage – this example was rated at 44 tons gross. But the state-owned British Road Services was looking for a 32 tons gross tractor to suit its own ideas, and Scammell collaborated, to produce many four-wheeled Crusaders. The same model was sold – in direct competition with Marathon – to other users, but in 1979 it was ended in order to make space at the Scammell works for Marathon, then displaced from AEC.

One of the few joint products of AEC and its new master was a family of rear-engined single deckers, intended mainly for bus work. With Leyland engines and transmissions they were Panthers; with AEC components they were Swifts, sometimes called Merlins. So much weight hanging from the chassis frame tail led to troubles with body flexing in both marques, and a host of engine failures gave the AECs a generally poor name. It was particularly sad that London Transport, begetter of AEC, should make the most emphatic rejection of this last all-new Southall bus: a fleet of about 1,500 were disposed of before reaching their first overhaul.

Left and below: For most of the 1970s the British Leyland companies received nothing but bad publicity. The company had caught popular imagination as a hopeless 'ne'er do well', and any good news of its affairs was usually suppressed. It was an unenviable position, particularly for the Truck and Bus division, which shared the odium heaped so liberally on the car plants. During this period Workington sought to create some favourable news by building special vehicles based on largely standard National body shells. There was a mobile bank, and an ambulance – and this 'Business Commuter', which in addition to a few very comfortable seats provided workspace for secretaries. As a publicity exercise it worked well, especially promotions outdoors.

Left: For three decades after 1945 the major preoccupation of nearly every motor works was how to increase output. In the circumstances wholesale reorganisations were difficult to the point of impossibility: how could the lines be stopped long enough? The Cowley plant of Morris Motors, then BMC, were in similar plight to the rest, and this Minor pick-up, being assembled next to a Wolseley saloon, is a graphic illustration of why modern, uncluttered, single product motor factories can so easily outpace the traditional kind. BLMC found itself in ownership of too many of the latter sort, and for practical purposes none of the former.

Quite possibly the saving of Scammell resulted from its inclusion in the British Leyland Motor Corporation Construction Equipment group of subsidiaries, where it was at least partially sheltered from the buffetings that assailed Truck and Bus. Other BL companies made rigid eight-wheelers, but increasingly during the lean years it was the Scammell Routeman which upheld the group's share in this important domestic market. The Routeman was peculiarly well suited to the building and civil engineering industries, and in tipper form particularly it proved to be long lived. Even in such rough work the exotically styled plastics cab lasted very well indeed.

enterprises. For too long, far too long, the old names were allowed to continue. Albion, Morris, Guy, Daimler, and the rest soldiered on for years after their ultimate control had passed into rival hands, and they inevitably attracted that fierce and misplaced loyalty that is always generated by lost causes.

It is often forgotten that factories and brand names are only half the story. Quite as important are the – usually – independent companies which actually sell vehicles and provide service and repair facilities for them. These distributors and dealers can be very large businesses indeed, and a major preoccupation for any manufacturer is creating and maintaining a high quality network of them. Despite the strong emphasis always placed on the need for network-wide 'corporate identity' the independence of these concerns most certainly extends to responsibility for their own financial welfare, something that comes much to the fore at times when manufacturer fortunes are in a state of flux.

This factor introduced yet more unwelcome complications into the developing British Leyland story, for as rationalisation of models and selling policies progressed, releasing dealers from old loyalties, the new importers were waiting to snap them up. It was, in its way, a striking illustration of the baffling problems facing BL company management during the hectic 1970s: rapid progress toward product and administrative coherency was an urgent necessity, yet the process must inevitably hand to powerful competitors the means of increasing that competition. Human nature being what it is valuable members of staff, attracted by the challenge of setting up new businesses, could also be tempted to change loyalties. Customers too, irked at the disappearance of makes they had favoured for years, were willing to take their custom elsewhere.

It was all a far cry from the days when those once-proud and now disappearing names first began to trade, although the origins of the companies were as diverse as their products. AEC

began as the maintenance offshoot of a bus operator; Crossley was once a branch of an engine maker. Wolseley had made sheep-shearing machines and Morris mended bicycles. Bicycles figured largely in early motoring history, Rover for one and Star for another starting in that way, but Marshall and Clayton were old-established agricultural and steam power engineers long before they built their first roadgoing vehicles. Leyland itself began as nothing grander than a village blacksmith. Of those which were founded as makers of motor vehicles Albion, Austin, Scammell, and Guy were prominent among the ones which guessed correctly and had nothing to do with steam. Indeed it is noticeable that the companies which avoided steam power tended to be the ones which prospered more often and lasted longest.

Broadly, too, the companies which balanced their books more often than not were the ones which concentrated heavily on bus production. Both Bristol and AEC, with related businesses,

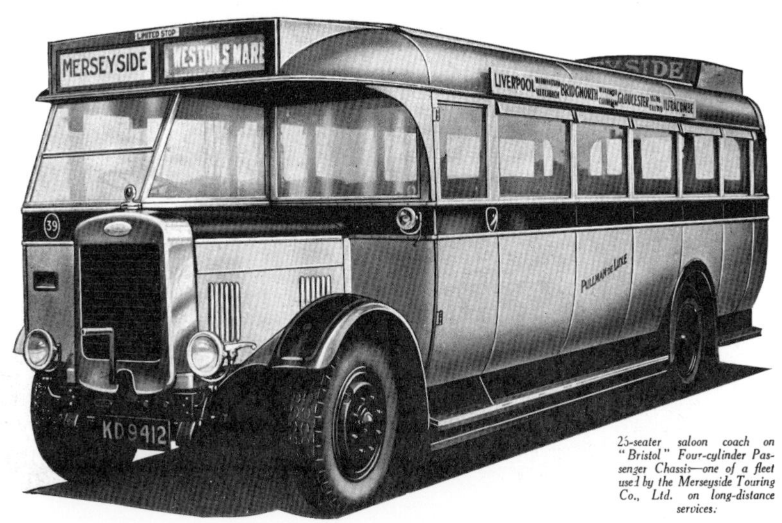

25-seater saloon coach on "Bristol" Four-cylinder Passenger Chassis—one of a fleet used by the Merseyside Touring Co., Ltd. on long-distance services.

Bodybuilder C.H. Roe had already passed into Park Royal control, in the late 1940s, before they both joined AEC in its new Associated Commercial Vehicles group. They were essentially bus constructors although, as the picture (**below**) shows, Park Royal skills were such as to appeal to the makers of Bristol cars. The rear-engined bus being bodied in the background is confirmation that despite the close ties with AEC, other makes of chassis were willingly bodied. **Above:** In one of its few essays in coach design, this Albion-mounted Royalist Viking of 1960, Park Royal showed that its styling was ten years ahead of competitors, but the result did not sell. The works finally closed as a result of an in-company quarrel over who would make the Titan double decker.

lived sheltered existences as favoured suppliers to very large operators. To a lesser extent, and informally, Daimler and Leyland also enjoyed the stability that came from possessing many steady customers, all of whom bought large fleets and paid their bills. It was no coincidence that the decline of these bus specialists ran closely parallel to the catastrophic general decline in bus usage, when car ownership became general in the 1950s and 1960s.

Those concerns which hitched their stars to export trading soon learned that disappointment was their most certain reward. When the Russian and Austro-Hungarian empires collapsed after the First World War they took with them enormous unsecured debts to many British makers of steam tackle, thereby fatally undermining post-war attempts to re-establish these businesses in more profitable lines. Much of the good work expended in penetrating the British Empire and other markets was arbitrarily destroyed at the outbreak of the next war in 1939 when, understandably enough, the British government effectively commandeered all output in the interests of the war

effort. It is hardly remembered now that with considerable enterprise Leyland, before 1939, had built up a worthwhile business in Canada. Thornycroft and Albion did well in Australia and Guy in South Africa. AEC made several South American cities its own. During that post-1945 vehicle famine some of the old markets, along with new ones, returned, but the years of wartime and post-war product shortage had let others establish themselves.

And it has to be said that all too often, in overseas markets, British manufacturers found their chief competitors among themselves. While these companies weakened each other in fighting for limited market shares, rivals from continental Europe, America, and latterly Japan quietly moved in and established selling networks from which they could not easily be dislodged. One of the more telling arguments put forward for merging AEC and Leyland, and before them Morris and Austin, was the pointlessness of such untrammelled competition. When the mergers eventually came, there came also the old familiar conundrums set by dealer, staff and customer loyalties, framed this time by the added difficulties of negotiations having to be made in foreign countries. Nor were matters helped during those trying times by the very attractive financing terms that could be offered by government-encouraged foreign competitors – backing hardly available to British manufacturers.

Above and above left: The distinctive cab adopted by BMC in 1960 for its FG range of chassis was successful on several counts: it was in its day considered comfortable; was distinctive; and, except for the portliest of drivers, the narrow width and corner doors gave ready access even in traffic-saturated high streets and factory yards. Perhaps distinction went too far when it was fitted over engines too long for it. But although bought in large numbers for use by van salesmen, particularly those employed by chain bakeries, the design gradually became obsolescent. Like so many other products of BMC and BLMC the clever FG cab was starved of development resources, when it could have gone further.

Left: Following the 1960s changes in construction and use laws for vehicles in Britain there was a short-lived requirement for twin-steer artic tractors. Of those produced within the Leyland Motor Corporation only the Scammell Trunker was specifically designed for the work: the AEC Mammoth Minor and this Leyland Steer were modified versions of other chassis. These two latter did not last long – but while they did, they provided distracting competition within the group which could be justified only by asserting that customers were being given an opportunity to choose a favourite make. Yet the provision of such choice did little to prepare the warring parties for an increasingly difficult future.

Mergers

With so much emphasis during recent years upon motor industry mergers, it might easily be thought that such things are essentially a modern phenomenon, never before experienced. In fact the roots of the great Coming Together of the 1970s can be traced back to the very first companies during their formative years.

But, apart from those earliest essays in financial manipulation, commercial imprudence, unsaleable products, and sheer bad luck it can now be seen that the periods of greatest merger activity for vehicle makers were the two major industrial crises of the western world; in other words, the 1930s and the 1970s. And it is not particularly comforting to reflect that the British motor industry has been accompanied in these travails by its competitors in other western countries. It is questionable too whether on the whole they profited from their takeovers much more than the British from theirs, because at the root of most such mergers lies productive over-capacity of the industry as a whole: all it needs, in an erstwhile balanced sector of the market, is for one company to invest in new and therefore almost certainly more efficient production facilities. The new plant, once its teething troubles are overcome, will either produce more vehicles to be sold, which can be done only by increasing the maker's share of the market, or (less probably) the same number of vehicles at less cost each. Of course it is open to others to do likewise, provided they can raise sufficient money, and while national economies are expanding and there is growing demand for transport all may be well. When that demand slackens, or in time of slump disappears, motor manufacturers are left with factories that are producing fewer vehicles than is economic. Since some nations take a broader view than others of what constitutes international trade it follows that something very close to dumping, or selling abroad at unrealistic prices, can easily result. A steady chorus of complaints, rising to deafening levels from the mid-1960s, about such practices has long been a characteristic of the native British motor industry.

Such is the perversity of life that a company may just as easily find itself in impossible trading conditions which have been created by a boom in general industry. A sudden surge in demand that cannot be met from existing factories can all too easily lead to fat order books and customers waiting long periods for vehicles needed immediately. Market forces will soon arrange for rival makers to fill the gap, and customers lost in this way are not easily regained. Leyland group companies have had their fair share of both kinds of supply problems, and suffered accordingly; they have also inevitably been involved in the resultant mergings of hitherto rival interests. It is not altogether cynical to wonder what benefits have resulted for the apparent victors in amalgamations: certainly shareholders in the victims have received something for their pains, but the usual outcome sooner or later in most takeovers is that product ranges become 'rationalised', factories are 'streamlined', and dealer networks 'reshaped'. More directly expressed, one partner has bought the other's place in the market, or bought off a troublesome competitor.

A third reason, and on the whole a sounder one, for joining forces is the desire of a company to secure its supplies. Not since the most primitive of early days have vehicle producers actually made all the parts of all their vehicles. The obvious exceptions are tyres, glass, and electrics, but as materials techniques advanced so rapidly it soon became possible for specialist suppliers to outdistance in-house facilities for research and development. In some cases a vehicle maker had

As the First World War receded, Crossley found itself with two main activities: a range of high quality motor cars, and development work on military vehicles. In an effort to widen its trading base the company entered into an agreement which gave it access to engines and transmissions supplied by the American Willys-Overland concern, and vehicles incorporating these items were marketed by Crossley as Willys-Overland-Crossley. Later, British-origin components were also used, and the Manchester name adopted, but by 1930 competition in the lightweight market was too intense and the enterprise foundered, leaving the original Crossley business still intact.

The British Alvis company was essentially a maker of sporting and high class passenger cars, and inevitably from time to time light van bodywork was mounted on Alvis chassis. Then during the 1960s the company produced a close-coupled high mobility six-wheeled chassis for military and similar purposes. There were armoured car versions, personnel carriers, fire crash tenders for airport work, and, as this picture shows, load carriers, of about 5 tons capacity. Civilian versions were made, but little came of it. Alvis joined Rover in 1965, and with Rover the Leyland Motor Corporation. Later, BLMC sold it.

Above left: Despite fierce competition in almost every other sphere, AEC and Leyland recognised that the post-1945 demand for trolleybuses would not be great, and that their best interests might be served by joining forces. The result was British United Traction – BUT – and products were marketed jointly, although in the main they comprised distinctively AEC or Leyland designs. Chassis were produced in the main Leyland plant and also another at Ham in Surrey; AEC built them at Southall and also in Crossley, by then its ACV-group subsidiary. The last ones were made at the Scammell plant. Few trolleybuses used in Britain were single-decked: Cardiff had to contend with low bridges.

Above: A clear indication of the future for Britain's motor industry was the Leyland purchase of Standard Triumph International, and this loaded transporter carries a representative selection of STI products at the time the company succumbed. STI was essentially a volume car maker, and its boldest venture in the way of commercial vehicles was the Atlas, here in van form. Leyland later used the Atlas front end for the Scarab Four, a shortlived urban artic by Scammell. The Vista Vue cab fitted to this Leyland transporter was also used by Scammell, Albion, and Brossel – the Belgian concern which after a long period of independence, became part of British Leyland.

Below: Bean was an unusual concern in that it was essentially a components maker which wanted to build vehicles – usually the reverse applied. It acquired the rights to a passenger car design, and also produced light vans based on the same chassis; later, heavier purpose-built commercial vehicles were made. In all its enterprises it committed the fatal error of attempting to wrest market shares away from such as Morris, and the American and European importers; in such competition Bean was no competition. Yet another in a long succession of reorganisations took the firm back to component making, and it is as such that it survives still within the BL group.

Although never a noticeably prosperous one, the Maudslay life was long and charmed. The firm began in 1903 with cars and soon turned also to commercial vehicles: generally its designs echoed what was being done by others, a sensible course for a small manufacturer. In their personal capacities Maudslay directors also had interests in Rover and Standard – a Maudslay family member founded the latter – and Rover made some Maudslay lorries during the First World War. During the late 1940s the company prudently threw in its lot with AEC, gave up its own distinctive models, including this Marathon coach, and turned to building specials for its parent.

A marked characteristic of the merged Austin and Nuffield empires was the adoption of much 'badge engineering', in which products from one partner were sold – and registered – bearing the other name, and sometimes with both names. The usual reason was the need to be even-handed with two separate and competing dealer networks, but the practice led to some curious results. These vehicles, clearly from the Nuffield, or Morris, factory were part of a large Austin-only display and therefore carried Austin badging. But a hint of things to come are the 'BMC diesel' badges, just under the windscreens.

It is curious that although the reverse is often true, engine makers have rarely translated into vehicle builders. Crossley tried: it was a much-respected maker of internal combustion engines of all kinds and in the early years supplied engines to vehicle makers. It is, therefore, doubly curious that when diesel engines became fashionable Crossley Motors proved unable to design and build a successful unit of its own. Its persistence in trying fatally weakened the firm, and it disappeared into AEC almost without trace. This late double decker has a Crossley body, an effective design which was no commercial match of the Roe and Park Royal products also offered by AEC, though its bodybuilding division continued after chassis production ceased.

Bristol had the good fortune to spend much of its life under the wings of friendly operators. It began as a branch of the Bristol Tramways and Carriage Company and joined, with its parent, the once-great Tilling group of companies. Within the group it partnered Eastern Coach Works, a fellow subsidiary; when Tilling fell into state ownership during the late 1940s Bristol and ECW sales were limited to state-owned fleets. Later Leyland took a share in both and ultimately BLMC assumed control. (State-owned ECW made some chassisless buses.) Convention was the hallmark of Bristol vehicles, and its only enduring novelty was the low height Lodekka, left and centre.

Thornycroft began as an offshoot of a Thames-side builder of steam launches and gunboats, and after early dalliance with steam power soon adopted petrol and paraffin engines for its road vehicles. The maritime connection took Thornycroft all over the world, and the motor factory soon developed an export trade that was envied by many. Although the steamers were made under licence in America, Germany, and Scotland, Thornycroft had little need of alliances with other firms until the 1950s when it lost the will to live. A measure of its plight was the decision in 1961 to sell to AEC, by then in a bad way itself. Most Thornycroft lorries of the 1920s, like this 5-6 tonner, were very ugly.

Trojan began as a good idea looking for a home: Leyland at the time wanted a passenger car. Thus it was, with Leyland as a somewhat unlikely parent, that the idiosyncratic Trojan grew into maturity. Trojans were meant to be simple machines, bringing motoring to the masses. Unfortunately most people looked askance on the odd two-stroke engines and solid rubber tyres, but the Trojan was found to be an ideal base for light urban delivery vans. It also proved irresistable to experimenters, and towards the end of Leyland ownership in 1928 this cross-country six-wheeler was made. Trojan then moved out of its Kingston factory, leaving production space for the Leyland Cub.

Austin was for many years essentially a car maker, although there was, early on, a strange and commercially unsuccessful lorry or bus chassis which incorporated twin drive shafts and a radiator mounted behind its engine. Thereafter Austin left heavier vehicles alone, and this half-ton van is an excellent example of an Austin light van of the early 1930s. Then, at the end of the decade, the decision was made to build American (and Morris) style medium weight chassis; they were successful, and the dominant role of Austin in the BMC combine was reflected by the combined Austin-Morris Commercial range of products. And also, therefore, of BLMC medium weight chassis.

been no more than an assembler of parts made elsewhere under contract. But the great drawback to sharing with others the services of an independent supplier is an inherent risk that something may happen to persuade that supplier to cut off supplies, or to demonstrate his independence in other unwelcome ways. Perhaps financial ruin and bankruptcy stare him in the face, or another client shows signs of wishing to acquire the business. At all events, a time comes when the customer wishes to be a customer no more but to turn proprietor instead.

It was in this way that what became the Nuffield group of companies grew, for William Morris bought his sub-assemblies from many suppliers. Later, as funds and opportunity permitted, he also acquired the companies as well. In a factory once owned by transmissions supplier Wrigley the Morris Commercial enterprise was set up and won success, and in premises built by Wolseley, in 1927 another of the Morris bargain buys, the 1930s range of heavy lorries and buses were made. In the years when Wolseley, later Wolseley Siddeley, had made commercial vehicles it was owned by Vickers – and was in its earliest days managed by Herbert Austin. Stellite, which once long ago made a light van, was effectively a subsidary of Wolseley. The Morris engine division was founded on Hotchkiss, a French-origin concern that was previously a supplier to Morris, and became so to Morris-Leon Bollee, when for a few years in the 1920s, the future Lord Nuffield made an unsuccessful attempt to enter continental Europe.

Herbert Austin exemplified the other way of doing things – of making as many components as possible under his own roofs. This was probably necessary: he started well before Morris, at a time when component suppliers as such hardly existed, and he was catering for higher price brackets, which implied far lower production. However, by the time that the Austin and Morris empires finally came together in 1952 to form the British Motor Corporation both were essentially manufacturers. It was a merger soured by abrasive relationships between individuals in the two companies and was sadly typical of other motor industry amalgamations. It could have happened

any time during the previous three decades – when, in all probability, the Morris (or Nuffield) half would have been dominant. As it was the Austin component took charge, although the rapid fusing of commercial vehicle designs into a more or less rational production programme was for several years one of the few positive signs of the merger. That programme was entirely devoted to light and medium weight goods vehicles; passenger service vehicles figured hardly at all and at a time when legally permissible vehicle weights were steadily increasing the BMC was too deeply embroiled in its volume car businesses to take much action. So from the somewhat narrow viewpoint of lorry and bus interests there was logic in the 1967 takeover by British Motor Holdings (formed by BMC in the previous year) of: Jaguar, since Jaguar had in 1960 possessed itself of Daimler, makers of a double-decked bus that challenged Leyland; Guy (1962) which had a line of saleable heavy trucks on its drawing boards; and specialist Henry Meadows (1964), next-door neighbour to Guy and by then depending upon a dwindling general market for its heavy engines. BSA, the previous owner of Daimler, was no longer willing to devote money to making luxury cars and a limited range of buses; Guy had simply drifted to a standstill, and Meadows turned out not to be an asset to its new owners.

BMC made most of the components it built into complete commercial vehicles – Daimler and Guy had become assemblers. In early times most makers of medium and heavy chassis had been largely self-sufficient, but as the years went by it became all too clear that commercial and technical success lay in the ability to produce components in huge quantities, enough and more than enough to finance research and development. Very few 'own source' makers could consume their own products at a sufficiently high rate (which was a powerful incentive for the more successful ones to sell to companies which apparently were competitors, and for firms like Austin and Morris not to move away from high sales volume light and medium products into low selling heavies), and so many came gradually to depend upon outside makers of engines, axles,

Above: 'Cost plus' is a comfortable way of pricing, but it can undermine the competitive spirit. This helps to explain the success of AEC in making excellent vehicles but sometimes less than pleasing financial results; with London as a largely captive customer the vehicles had to be good, but cost was almost secondary. The latter factor showed itself in overseas markets, where often Leyland charged less and made more profit. After 1945 AEC tried to become truly independent, and built a group that could have dominated commercial vehicle manufacture in Britain: but the Bridgemaster, a late essay at excellence, showed the old design flair had gone.

Top left: The National project was meant to usher in several new eras. It was to mark the transition from double to single-decked operation in Britain; it was to introduce almost car-style methods of manufacture; and not least it was to mark a new kind of partnership between operator and manufacturer, for the Leyland National Company Ltd was jointly owned by British Leyland and the State-controlled National Bus Company. In the event, the only enduring aspect of the National proved to be the quality of its design coupled with manufacturing methods which have yet to be equalled anywhere else. And National is now owned by Leyland Vehicles.

Above: After devouring Coulthard, one of its parents, in 1907, the Lancashire Steam Motor Company changed its name to Leyland Motors and took to a life of self-sufficiency, in which the acquisition of Trojan in 1922 was an uncharacteristic highlight. Leyland, seeing that in the post-1945 years sheer size would be essential to survival, bought Albion. Then came Scammell, taking Leyland into new fields, and Standard Triumph, a car maker. From then on merger momentum became too fast for comfort. This Titan, typically a Leyland of the 1930s, carries an Eastern Coach Works body, and thereby presages one of the last of a long line of mergers.

Below left: The Glasgow Motor Lorry Company (whose products were occasionally sold as Glasgows) soon saw the wisdom of abandoning steam power, thereupon adopting the name of its founder in the title Halley's Industrial Motors. In its day it made a wide range of heavy vehicles – including fire appliances and double-decked buses – but it had a weakness for expensive experimental engineering. This was a luxury that could be ill-afforded in the 1920s and after several financial crises Halley closed its doors in 1935. Its products were well made but, as this c 1930 van shows, conservative in design. Albion bought the company.

Below: Apart from the occasional car-derived light van, the Rover company did not often find itself involved with commercial vehicles. Until, that is, in post-1945 Britain, when the company was compelled to find a product that could be exported. It hit upon the idea of a light four-wheel-drive car-cum-tractor with which farmers could plough, or take their pigs to market. Land-Rover was the obvious and happy title for the project, and the rest is common knowledge. The Land-Rover and its potential was a major factor in persuading the Leyland Motor Corporation to take it under its wing; now it seems the 'go anywhere' vehicle will become the sole legacy of the old Rover company.

Top left: For nearly all of its life Guy managed to combine high quality hand-assembled engineering with keen pricing. Ultimately the tightrope became too narrow, and Guy fell into the arms of Jaguar. A prime cause of the final collapse was Wulfrunian, this double-decked bus of advanced but ill-developed design which sapped company finances. Sydney Guy had worked for Sunbeam before starting his own business, so it was fitting that in 1948 he should buy the Sunbeam trolley bus rights. Star had long since been absorbed. Under the Jaguar wing Guy and Daimler were just beginning to rationalise models and components. Then came BMH, and British Leyland.

Top right: William Morris rapidly rose to the dominant position among British car makers, despite some powerful opposition, notably from foreign companies. By 1924 he was looking for new fields for expansion and, patriotically scenting a profit, decided to tackle the importers of light commercials. This very early van was simply a 'Morris', but soon a separate company, Morris Commercial Cars, was set up to exploit the potential. The car company continued to market car-derived light vans, and both were part of Nuffield, the Morris holding company. After the merger with Austin, commercial vehicle design was rationalised, but the Morris name lived on until BLMC days.

Above: The London General Omnibus Company, a giant of its kind, found itself desperate for reliable vehicles and resolved to build its own. Some expertise had been acquired together with rival companies, and by 1910 the immortal B-type had evolved. Early specimens bore the name 'General', or 'LGOC', on their radiators but in 1912 the bus factory was established as a separate entity trading as the Associated Equipment Company. The M.E.T. fleet name on the side of this B-type reflected a convoluted chain of events in which, as part compensation for a cancelled London fleet order, Daimler agreed to sell AEC products, and AEC built chassis for Daimler.

and other higher technology items. The logic of this state of affairs became inescapable to everyone concerned. Once customers fully appreciated that they were being invited to buy the same limited selection of components assembled into similar configurations by any of a large number of 'manufacturers', it was inevitable that considerations other than technical excellence would affect buying decisions. Initial price and after-sales service became dominating factors, and in that sort of climate big companies get bigger, and small ones fade away.

The demise of Halley serves to illustrate this pattern of events, though it could be said that in a sense this old established concern continued as part of the Albion manufacturing facilities. Albion was very much a manufacturer rather than an assembler and survived longer than most because its products were well designed and made, and its customers were not of the kind which demand frequent model changes. Even so when ultimately the company was acquired by Leyland in 1951 a prime reason was the need for added financial and technical resources of the kind available only within a large grouping. Distinctively Albion models continued for some years, although with an increasingly Leyland tinge to them, but now the factory has itself turned exclusively component maker, producing axles and gearboxes. Scammell, the other notable chassis maker acquired by (1955) Leyland Motors, has by means of sturdy rearguard action preserved a recognisable identity for itself and its products, but both are heavily influenced by Leyland and neither are likely to have survived outside of a major protective grouping.

Standard, more properly Standard Triumph International, was essentially a volume car and light van maker which became available in 1961 just at the time that Leyland felt it needed a major presence in the passenger car business. In its own circle of competitors STI had become outclassed in the race to gain corporate size despite a steady programme of acquisitions, most of whom were previously suppliers. Of these perhaps the most significant was Bean, a components maker which for a time in the years between

Pre-1914 Daimlers were heavily influenced by two factors: the specifications laid down by the British government for vehicles that would be eligible for subsidy, and the association with AEC. There were, therefore, many points of similarity between chassis sold by the two companies – indeed, some were identical. One important shared detail was a wooden chassis frame, comprised of planks of ash sandwiched between thin steel plates, but although durable and effective the idea was not original. The impossibility of making a drop-frame by this method hardly mattered before the mid-1920s, and this Daimler of about 1912 carries the high floored tram-style bodywork of its period.

the wars had made a range of unsuccessful cars and light commercials. During that period Bean in turn had owned among others Vulcan, a concern which eked out a precarious existence largely in commercial vehicle manufacture and which in time passed into other hands. The Triumph component of STI also had its vicissitudes and several previous owners but kept in the main to the more sporting kinds of passenger car. The Standard name, soon no doubt to become quite forgotten in Britain, lives on in India where the independent Standard Motor Products still makes light commercials, while Bean blossomed anew as a division within British Leyland.

The event which showed most clearly where the future would lie was the takeover by Leyland of Associated Commercial Vehicles. Despite always apparent and often real prosperity the AEC had often found itself looking for business partners, with two serious attempts to link with Daimler, and at least two with Leyland – the British United Traction joint venture of 1946 to make trolley buses and railcars being the tangible outcome of one. (BUT is remembered in the title of British Leyland group components supplier SU-Butec, which recalls also a carburettor maker once bought by Morris.) Then, perhaps despairing of finding a partner among equals, AEC bought Crossley and Maudslay, both of which had long histories of at best partial success, and with them formed ACV.

In an attempt soon after the First World War to widen its scope the Crossley company set up a separate concern called Willys-Overland-Crossley which assembled and adapted light commercials designed by the American Willys-Overland company: some later versions were marketed as Manchesters, but the enterprise foundered when the American partner went out of business. Maudslay, whole origins despite misleading publicity by ACV did not go back to the 1830s, failed to attract any partners, although there were at times personal financial links between its directors and both Standard and Rover. Within a few years ACV had closed Crossley without trace but the Maudslay plant lived on and indeed does still, although sold out of

the Leyland group some years ago and now concentrating on making drive axles for Rockwell. Specialist bus bodybuilders Park Royal and Charles H. Roe, already linked, joined AEC soon after Crossley and Maudslay and were probably better bargains than either – or even Thornycroft, which joined ACV in 1961 and rapidly became hardly more than an outwork station. It too was sold out of the group by Leyland and became part of the Eaton Corporation, who are transmission specialists. By the time Thornycroft threw in its lot with ACV the group as a whole was in a bad way, and in efforts to avoid the inevitable asked British Motor Holdings to consider a merger. Rolls-Royce, a year or two earlier, had already refused a similar plea. In 1962 came the offer that couldn't be refused, and Leyland took control.

Although fully aware of the virtue, or at least necessity, of size it may be questioned whether Leyland itself was really merger-minded. Albion, Scammell, and Leyland Motors were still clearly identifiable entities in 1962, and the process of reinvigorating Standard Triumph had hardly begun. What soon became clear was that the group had not provided itself with enough senior managers of a calibre to handle the problems now facing it, and the acquisition of ACV merely added to this worry. Yet for several good reasons, not the least of which was a great deal of anti-Leyland sentiment in the AEC camp, the time had come to weld the whole unwieldy structure of the new Leyland Motor Corporation (1963) into one clearly identifiable concern. Given time it might easily have succeeded, but time was something in short supply. During these momentous years for the companies which had traditionally comprised the British heavy vehicle industry, BMH, with undigested takeovers of its own and still almost entirely dependent on the increasingly volatile and unpredictable volume car market, slid inexorably into great danger. By common consent it could no longer survive alone, and by 1968 there was only one credible partner: Leyland. It was a poor foundation for the great coming together, but still the mergers continued. Rover had entered the LMC in 1967; Aveling Barford (bringing with it associates making bridges and concrete mixers) in 1968; and in 1975 the ailing Marshall came into the fold. The state-owned Bristol and its Eastern Coach Works partner became associates controlled by the new British Leyland Motor Corporation, which handed a share in Park Royal-Roe to the Government as part of a new bus building consortium, National Bus.

When the Corporation was formed in May 1968 it merged the LMC and BMH into what was probably the second largest motor manufacturer in Europe, and the fifth largest in the world. It was responsible for forty major manufacturing plants in Britain and another seventy subsidiaries and assemblers overseas.

To make the problems involved comprehensible, the whole was split into seven divisions, each huge, and bringing together in rational groupings companies which, often, had previously little in common with each other. The volume car business continued to falter and the oil crisis of 1973 dealt several serious blows.

The whole could not possibly succeed and it did not. The 1970s saw frequent intervention by government in one crisis after another until finally time, money, and patience all became exhausted.

Opposite top: Star became yet another example of a company that started early and well in motor manufacturing but which failed to weather that lethal late 1920s/early 1930s combination of international slump and rapidly changing requirements by users. Star made a well regarded range of cars, and therefore light vans on car chassis; commercial vehicles proper were made from before the First World War; later the company took its philosophy of light, fast, and well made vehicles into medium weight buses and lorries. But Star was a low volume producer at a time when mass-production was taking over. The company, bought by Guy in 1928, was soon gone without trace.

Opposite bottom: The Daimler name proved to have remarkable durability, and it was of considerable help to the company in combining as well as it did the manufacture of expensive luxury cars with lorries and buses. Apart from the two well-known attempts to form joint operating companies with AEC, Daimler continued its largely independent path within the BSA group of companies, until the 1950s showed that for this relatively small maker time too had run out. Jaguar, keen to build its own empire, bought Daimler; then BMH bought Jaguar; and LMC bought BMH. The last of a long line of interesting Daimlers were the Fleetlines, and the last Fleetlines were sold as Leylands.

Marshall Sons and Company was another of the remarkable steam engineers produced by the mid-19th century – and East Anglia. For many years it was huge, making vast quantities of agricultural equipment, boilers, and stationary steam engines and exporting them all over the world. Inevitably it also made self-moving engines, mainly for farm work but also for road haulage. This tractor was built in 1919. When Clayton and Shuttleworth, a similar concern, finally failed in 1930, Marshall acquired the goodwill. Later it merged with Fowler, yet another steam giant of old, and when it joined BLMC, becoming Aveling Marshall, it was the sole British-owned maker of tracked vehicles.

Name changes

Hardly any of the companies now part of British Leyland lasted their separate lives without major name changes – and in view of the changes that took place in their developments over the years that is hardly surprising. Some of them, however, seem almost to have made a pastime of reidentifying themselves and their products.

Leyland Motors was one of the steadier concerns, and settled down to that long-lived title in 1907. With minor variants it lasted until the merger with AEC and the creation of the Leyland Motor Corporation. Then, after the great merger with British Motor Holdings, there was a shortlived attempt to apply the Leyland name to everything from minicars upwards.

Leyland Motors was itself the outcome of a merger. Originally trading as the Lancashire Steam Motor Company, half of its capital had been found by T. Coulthard of Preston, not far from Leyland: Coulthard also made roadgoing steamers, and there was in addition a separate American Coulthard company in Boston, Mass. In 1907, however, Coulthard formally merged with the Lancashire Steam Motor Company to form Leyland Motors. But not before it had built two or three steam waggons for Dr. Brightmore. These strange machines, sometimes referred to as Brightmores, sometimes as Manchesters, were virtually articulated four-wheelers and so far outside conventional thinking that they met small response; Coulthard was no doubt wise in not putting its own name on to them. Leyland's enthusiasm for steam vehicles was short-lived but the company stayed in the market until 1926, when all its rights, spares, and drawings were handed over to Atkinson. This concern proceeded to follow its own eventful path, and seems unlikely to take any further part in the Leyland story.

The beginnings of AEC were more complicated, and were reflected in its name. It was in 1906 that the London Motor Omnibus Company, at its corporate wits' end with the chronic unreliability of early motor buses, resolved to build its own. Some MOCs – Motor Omnibus Construction – were made using proprietary parts, and when these two linked concerns merged with the much larger London General Omnibus Company in 1908 chassis production continued. In 1912 the General set its sights on supplying buses to other operators and hived off its factory under the appropriate title Associated Equipment Company.

Long after the original association had been forgotten the initials AEC lived on, although to the company's annoyance it was forced away from them in certain markets, notably South America and Spain, where the German AEG company insisted that confusion could result and claimed prior rights. Hence, although AEG was essentially a maker of heavy electrical equipment, and hardly more than dabbled in road vehicles, AEC had to adopt the light disguise of ACLO, or Associated Company London Omnibuses. Later, however, AEC became involved in a curious and uncharac-

teristic enterprise when, under the influence of its manager, George Rushton, agricultural type tractors were made at the AEC works. Some of these had General cast into their radiators, and some Rushton. Equally odd but longer lasting was the Hardy connection: Hardy Rail Motors began as an associate of the resoundingly titled British Four-Wheel-Drive Tractor Lorry Super-Engineering Company, earlier the British Four-Wheel-Drive Tractor Lorry Company, which in turn had stemmed from British Quad. This concern was set up during the First World War to make four-wheel drive lorries under licence from the American FWD company. By 1929 they had taken to using AEC major components, and it was therefore logical for them to become directly linked. For some years AEC used its own name, or Hardy, or both together, for the not-inconsiderable number of full-sized diesel railcars that it made, and Hardy-origin designs in due course of time became the famed AEC Matador gun tractors of the Second World War.

In contrast to this orderly progression AEC took part in a bizarre change of identity during 1936, when for a short while the company took an interest in the affairs of Sunbeam, while that concern was owned by the Rootes Group, and a Gardner-engined but otherwise quite standard AEC double-decked bus was sold as a Sunbeam.

The extraordinary thing about the Sunbeam company was not the frequency of changes in its name, but rather in its changes of owner. It began as a bicycle, then car, manufacturer in the earliest days of motor transport and decided in 1929 as the Sunbeam Motor Car Company that it could make an impression on the bus business. Unfortunately the impression was neither deep nor lasting, although the company did rather better in trolleybuses. In 1934 a separate firm, Sunbeam Commercial Vehicles, was set up and the next year both businesses were sold to the Rootes Group. Next, the Brockhouse general engineering group bought the Commercials part; and Guy took it on in 1949. Then, of course, Sunbeam went to Jaguar, BMH, and BLMC. During the period under Rootes control the trolleybus part of Karrier was welded on to Sunbeam, too.

Another Sunbeam activity during the late 1930s was in battery-electrics, seemingly a quiet and placid world but one in which strange things could happen. Sunbeam faded on the outbreak of war, but an almost unbelievably complicated series of name changes centred around the Morrison company, which in 1936 merged with the Electricar concern to form Associated Electric Vehicle Manufacturers. Electricar itself could include in its origins the great name of Edison, and also Electromobile, which had made some big vehicles. AEVM was bought by Crompton Parkinson in 1941 and, after the war had ended, Austin took a half-share in the business, which now became Austin Crompton Parkinson Electric Vehicles. In due course of time Crompton was bought by

Above: For many years Guy indiscriminately used the 'Arab' name for both double and single-decked bus chassis, and when the company introduced its own underfloor-engined single decker Arab was used again, thereby perhaps losing in confusion what it gained in consistency. Guy was a considerable exporter, and it early discovered and exploited a market in countries with poor roads for tough, go almost anywhere, buses which owed much to heavy duty lorry practice. One such vehicle was the Guy Victory, which did so well over many years that BLMC was happy to keep it in the group catalogue, labelling it, as in this West Indian sample, Leyland Victory.

Above: AEC and Daimler had collaborated before, but the nearest they ever came to merging was in 1926 when a new joint business, Associated Daimler Company, was established. AEC had by then made the decision to move to its brand-new factory at Southall, and the intention at that time was for chassis to be made there and fitted either with AEC poppet-valve engines or Daimler sleeve-valve units. Marketing was to be unified. Quite soon the centralised production plan faded, with some new models being built at Daimler, and after only two years the ADC was finished. Although largely a bus-building enterprise lorries were also made, including this 4-5 tonner of 1928.

Right: There was one drawback to the generally excellent Leyland scheme of model naming: the difficulty of finding suitable superlatives. The problem showed itself particularly in export markets where heavy duty versions rather clumsily became Super Beavers, Super Hippos, and so on. The company was inclined to use and reuse favoured bus names so that in 1950, when this heavily underfloor-engined chassis reached completion, Leyland was already using Tiger for its front-engined single deckers. The newcomer therefore became, as pictured here, Royal Tiger: then came the export Royal Tiger Worldmaster, as clumsy a label as any, but then Tiger Cub for a medium weight machine did much to redeem things.

Right: The Routemaster is a remarkable vehicle and probably the last in a long line of London peculiars – London designs for use in London and made in very large numbers. Preliminary design work began before the 1940s were out, production began in 1959, and when it did a new vehicle marque was created, Park Royal, which assembled AEC front and rear running units into the body shells. The 'master' theme went on to catch the imaginations of professional publicists in much the same way as 'mini'. A hand in pocket Lord Brabazon, then chairman of Associated Commercial Vehicles, is casting a quizzical gaze over Routemaster 1000, in October 1961.

Above: Considering the skill with which he used publicity in other directions, Morris was surprisingly unsure when it came to the important matter of naming his products, and there was some overlapping even between 'Morris' vans, made by the car factory, and the lightest models of the 'Morris Commercial' range. Generally the Morris Commercial business relied upon an uninspired system of model letters, and a confusion of Z, D, G, C, TX and similar types resulted. Then during the 1930s William Morris clearly showed where his sympathies lay in a series of model names that included Imperial, Viceroy, Dictator, Director, Leader, Champion, and Courier. These are Leaders.

Left: The Sunbeam name might fairly be said to have led a charmed life, and over the years it has been applied to every kind of vehicle, including this trolley bus of the early 1930s. The variety of product was matched by a corresponding variety of owners, for Sunbeam was one of those concerns with potential – a potential which, somehow, never quite blossomed. One singular outcome was the simultaneous marketing of motor bikes, cars, and trolley buses, all bearing the Sunbeam name and all made by separate companies. At that time also Sunbeam was selling trolley

Scammell, lacking inspiration and with a sideways look at a direct rival named the Cob, called its three-wheeled urban tractor the Mechanical Horse – which, in many ways, was a perfect description, for some of the earliest ones were adapted to haul ex-horse vehicles. But horses of the flesh and blood kind, common in the early 1930s, were less so by the 1950s and with them much of the original significance of the name. So post-war Horses were called Scarabs, which at least had the merit of alliteration, and this last generation of all, before legislation helped exterminate the breed, were individually Townsman, and collectively (if a little uncertainly) Townsmen.

buses labelled as Karriers, when that name properly belonged to motor lorries made by others.

Above: Guy production was at a low ebb when finally its independence came to an end and Jaguar took control. Several of the old models continued in production for a while but in 1964 came the first – indeed, as events turned out the only – entirely new heavy truck of the new regime. With unassailable logic it was labelled simply the Big J range, and Big J4s, J6s, and J8s became common currency. Since the vehicles were built up largely from bought-in components it was possible to tailor specifications accurately to customer requirements, and the Big J in its several forms soldiered on well into BLMC days as a robust, uncomplicated, general purpose vehicle.

Above right: Despite some early – and late – variety in its model names AEC was much inclined to use and reuse old favourites. From the mid-1920s there was a leaning toward the initial letter R, with Ramillies, Reliance, Regal, Ranger (well suited to a chassis meant mainly for touring coach work), Renown, and Regent – although the latter, implying a temporary substitute for something grander, was an odd choice in a contemporary market which included many rival makes and models. This Regent of the 1930s, like so many others before and since spent a long lifetime in the service of London Transport, by then in the nature of a cousin to AEC, despite joint parentage.

Hawker Siddeley, which already owned Brush, a company that made battery-electrics in addition to other kinds of electrical equipment. Finally BL sold the Austin shareholding to Hawker Siddeley, too.

The Daimler name has proved to be remarkably durable, apart from minor adventures such as the shortlived Associated Daimler Company. The primary reason, no doubt, is that most people have a dim awareness that Gottlieb Daimler invented motor cars, or something of the sort, and the impression that it is a name to be spoken of in respectful tones has never quite been lost. Its value as a trademark has also given it a confusing history, and in addition to those users whose descendants are now Daimler-Benz of West Germany and Steyr-Daimler-Puch of Austria there were also two trading with the name in Britain. One, Milnes Daimler, thrived in the domestic bus market during the first years of the century; but as it was hardly more than an importer and body builder for the German product it ceased trading during the First World War. Interestingly, in 1923 Thornycroft turned its ener-gies to producing the prototypes of a heavy gun tractor suitable for use in India and it used components taken from similar machines made by the German Daimler and captured after the war.

The second Daimler concern has been a com-pany of vicissitudes, and lost its independence early when Birmingham Small Arms – BSA – took it over. There were the attempts to merge it with SEC, and, soon after the First World War, with Leyland Motors; over the years it has produced a remarkably varied range of products that at one

time ranged from cars for the Royal family to trolley buses. After the transfer to Jaguar, and then Leyland, the ultimate indignity came when its last distinctive product, the Fleetline bus, was relabelled the Leyland Fleetline.

The formation of British Motor Holdings had the effect of bringing together the businesses con-trolled by Jaguar and the British Motor Corpora-tion. Jaguar was a relative newcomer to the commercial vehicle scene, but although it never got round to devising an overall corporate identity soon showed it meant business with its Daimler and Guy subsidiaries. BMC on the other hand had held a sizeable share of the lorry market since its foundation and its main constituents, Austin and Nuffield, had been making lorries long before that. Austin was another company which contrived to get along without many changes of name and so was Morris, the dominant part of Nuffield. Austin chassis were sold as Austin, small Morrises – essentially the car-derived light vans – as Morris, and the heavier ones as Morris Commercial. For its post-1946 London-style taxi cab Nuffield adop-ted the badge name Oxford, although the vehicle was a Wolseley factory product. Apart from that Wolseley had given up the commercial vehicle business before its absorption into the Morris empire in 1927.

But from many years of stability while still separate entities the naming policy after Austin and Morris became one company was erratic. Largely because of the need to satisfy two still separate dealer networks, and the wish to reduce competition between its own products, the new BMC took to selling ex-Austin products as Morris, Morris as Austin, and sometimes did so simul-taneously. An early attempt to establish 'BMC' as a marque did not last long although it returned later. Meanwhile Austin-Morris and Mini became established in their own right. After the British Leyland Motor Corporation was formed the Ley-land name was put on to heavier ex-BMC chassis, and since then bewilderment has continued with such combinations as Freight Rover and Austin Rover, although Rover, which joined Leyland Motor Corporation in 1966, had, apart from its multi-purpose Land Rover, never been seriously engaged in commercial vehicles.

Scammell had a relatively uncomplicated his-tory, but for many years there was some con-fusion between it and another Scammell com-pany, and latterly with a third. Scammell Lorries Ltd was quite separate from, but a legitimate descendant of, G. Scammell and Nephew, the parting of the ways coming when the latter designed a highly successful articulated lorry which could only be satisfactorily produced by a separate company. Scammell and Nephew con-tinued independently, sinking ever deeper into successive mergers, until recent times – and on at least one occasion during the 1930s built a motor lorry of its own. Meanwhile Scammell Lorries, as a by-product of its main line of business, had established itself as a well-regarded maker of semi-trailers. The Leyland Motor Corporation split off this activity into a separate company which had difficulty finding a permanent home, and after it had rested for a while at the old

Below: Maudslay was strong on alliteration, and such was the variety, if not sales, of its products that it found good use for Masta, Montrose, Majestic, Meteor, Mogul, Mikado, Mentor, Militant, Marathon, Magna, Maharanee, Mustang, Meritor, and others. Some were appropriate, particularly Majestic and Magna for double-decked buses. The two of eastern origin appeared irrelevant, and high-ranking Indian ladies would not have been flattered by having a large and rather ugly articulated lorry named after them. This Militant was a wartime design, and with others in the list bequeathed its name to AEC models; Majestic had also been used by AEC long before the merger.

Above: To all appearances an abiding characteristic of the Thornycroft vehicle naming policy was whimsy: how else could one explain Cygnet for a full-sized single-decked bus, or Daring for a double decker, or Tartar, Bullfinch, Beautyride, Dragon, Jupiter, among many others, for the vast range of models that the company made? The clue lay in the other half of the Thornycroft business – building warships for the navies of the world, from which the commercial vehicle enterprise had originally sprung, and whose products supplied an almost endless number of names. This Sturdy was essentially a pre-1939 model revived under licence during the war years.

In view of its lifelong emblem of the red indian bust ('feathers in our cap', ran the slogan) the choice of Arab for both double and single-decked buses seemed odd, but it lasted a very long time. For its heavy lorries of the 1950s Guy adopted the somewhat desperate-sounding Goliath, Formidable and Warrior – the latter having some relevance to the Indian. This Invincible revived a double decker bus name of the 1920s.

Left: Guy was another which liked the idea of animal names, but since the best ones were used by Leyland it had to make recourse to the less satisfactory Vixen, Otter, Fox, Seal, Wolf, and Ant, none of which were suitable for heavy chassis.

Scammell managed to get by with few model names until after Leyland Motors took control. When it did finally personalise its ordinary road haulage vehicles a new family was created: Routeman for the rigid eight-wheelers, Highwayman for this bonneted articulated tractor (which mechanically owed much to the very first Scammells) and Handyman, a label better suited perhaps to a busy little runabout than to what was broadly a forward control Highwayman. In earlier times Scammell relied on general descriptions than specific names – Flexible Six-Wheeler, Light Six-Wheeler, and 12-tons Prime Mover, among them.

For most of its many years Daimler preserved a lofty disdain toward names for its buses and lorries: straightforward sets of code letters and numbers, capable of being remembered and interpreted by other than Daimler employees, sufficed. A notable break from tradition was the early 1950s Freeline (**opposite centre left**), a name which neatly drew attention to the almost completely unobstructed top surface of a new underfloor-engined bus chassis. When in this successor the engine moved rearwards Roadline was chosen, and there was a certain symmetry in coining Fleetline for the rear-engined double decker which proved such troublesome competition for the Leyland Atlantean. But, as the picture shows (**opposite top**), Leyland had the last word.

Opposite bottom left: Albion, with a wary eye on its important local markets, concentrated heavily on north British allusions for its vehicle model names. There were Claymores, Caledonians, and Reivers, while this Aberdonian marks an abiding interest by Albion in lightweight buses. Chieftain and Clansman were once Halley names, exhumed for further service. Then there was a series beginning with V – Viking, Valiant, Valkyrie, and Venturer. The practice, and the names, continued well into the British Leyland era, but as Albion designs became obsolete and increasingly superseded by products from elsewhere in the group, not only did the model names go, but so did that of Albion itself.

The badge engineering which characterised the rival selling organisations within both Austin and Morris for long after they had merged continued well into British Leyland days. Many models carried this group cab, but although it began life in the early 1960s as a BMC design the majority were sold bearing Austin or Morris nameplates. British Leyland suppressed those two labels and for a while marketed, through Leyland Truck and Bus, a range of 'BMC' products which, however, also carried the BLMC catherine wheel emblem. Finally honesty prevailed with plain, unadorned 'Leyland' on the cab fronts.

Thornycroft works, the business was sold out of the group to York Trailers, which continued to use the Scammell name.

In passing, the Scammell factory has also been involved with two other products that moved factory more often than is usual. One was the BUT trolley bus: not only did Leyland produce chassis in two of its own factories, while AEC made some in its own plant and also at the Crossley premises, but the last samples were put together by Scammell.

And when AEC designed a heavy off-road dumper it gave the job of making them to its Maudslay subsidiary, which by then was concentrating on heavy work and specials. From Maudslay the Dumptruck went to Thornycroft, when that concern joined AEC; and on the formation of BLMC it moved again, to Aveling Barford, which had already joined Leyland. Aveling in turn passed it on to Scammell.

Steady erosion of international, though not language, barriers in recent times has had the incidental effect of creating enormous difficulties within motor manufacturers for the people whose job it is to find suitable model names for new products. Too many simply take refuge in type numbers, and thereby deny a dull world of a little bit of colour: others use and reuse a limited collection of model names; some simply invent meaningless words which research has shown will not create offence in even the most obscure of languages or dialects. It is a difficult problem, and unstinted praise should go to the old Leyland Motors, which hit on the unrivalled scheme of

using animal names, and applying them logically in families. Thus the four-cylindered forward control single deck bus became the Lion, the normal control version the Lioness, and the smallest one the Lion Cub. When six cylinder engines became available so did Tigers and Tigresses. Among the lorries the busy-sounding Badger and Beaver were both medium-sized vehicles suitable for delivery work while the Rhino was large and ugly. Inevitably eight-wheelers were called Octopus, and when six-wheelers with two axles at the front came into fashion the result became the Steer. A light and rapid six-wheeler made during the 1920s and 1930s for military use, and which was much favoured by the Territorial Army, was the Terrier – perhaps the happiest choice of all.

Compared with this brilliance all the others paled into at best mere imitators. AEC for years used Regal and Regent for its single and double-decked buses, although they might have been more logical the other way round. Mammoth Major was applied to both six- and eight-wheeled chassis so indiscriminately and for so long that most people forgot there had once been, simply, a Mammoth – but there was, a middling-sized four-wheeler. For a short while much later there was a Mammoth Minor too. AEC also used Mustang and Militant, which it inherited from Maudslay along with Merlin and Mogul, but Reliance although no doubt apt has a dreary sound to it. So did the Austin Loadstar and Omnivan, and the Morris Commercial Equiload.

Thornycroft pursued lines of thought all its own in the matter of naming, and while Mighty Antar could hardly be bettered for the huge oilfield and army tank transporter which it made in the 1950s there was a slightly jokey sound to its slightly smaller brother, Big Ben. And at the lower end of the Thornycroft scale Sturdy, Beauty, Nippy, Trusty, and Dainty seemed better suited to cart horses than to lorries.

Further difficulties could easily result if a company allowed itself to indulge in bombast. The

Leyland Titanic six-wheeled double decker, in competition with its AEC rival the Renown, soon lived up to its namesake and sank. A later Leyland inspiration, Atlantean, seemed pointless to perhaps most of its buyers and users, who would not have known that the mythological Atlanteans were related to the equally fabled Titans. The family of 'masters' had mixed fortunes. It was founded by AEC-Park Royal with Routemaster, which proved to be so in London only. Leyland Worldmaster bus chassis did indeed secure an enviable place in export markets, but the closely related Firemaster fire appliance version was soon extinguished. Morris Commercial found its Leader bus was not so regarded by most potential buyers, and in choosing Dictator and Imperial as model names during the early 1930s showed a woeful myopia regarding current events. And perhaps the choice of New Era, by Bean, was merely pathetic: the company failed soon afterwards. At Guy the Invincible proved to be nothing of the kind while for its lighter models a feeble attempt to ape Leyland produced Wolf, Vixen, Otter, and the oddly cross-bred Vix-Ant.

When Albion took to product names it betrayed an essentially provincial outlook by choosing Reiver, Chieftain, Claymore, Caledonian, and others of similar kind – including the uninspired Lowlander for a lightly disguised Leyland Titan. There was also a timid-sounding Venturer. The nature of Scammell products made Pioneer, Mountaineer, and Constructor appropriate names, but the equally apt Sherpa suffered a strange transformation when Leyland took it from Scammell and applied it to an Austin-Morris light van. An obvious and accurate Scammell name was Mechanical Horse for its urban tractor, but Scarab seemed to have little relevance for the second generation Horses. The final version, Townsman, was however just right.

Curiously, one of the most prolific users of model names has turned out to be Fowler, a company which merged with Marshall in 1947 and is now hardly remembered, and not at all for the shortlived range of diesel lorries which it made during the 1930s. Yet among them were Marathon, to be used by Leyland for a stopgap model of the 1970s; Crusader, applied by Scammell to a successful range also of the 1970s; Leviathan, which had been used by Leyland for a rather small and not very successful double decker during the 1920s; Warrior, which came and went and came again with Guy; and Comet, which Leyland used for many years from the late 1940s onwards – although Comets produced in India were sometimes labelled Vikings, which had been an Albion name!

The Willys-Overland-Crossley, or Manchester, was a doomed attempt by car and bus builder Crossley to break into the volume light commercial market.

AD
48
BREWERS
SINCE
1742
BY APPOINTMENT

Common sourcing

Sound commercial reasons can lead to the coming together of strange bedfellows, and this is particularly so among heavy commercial vehicle makers, where total production numbers are often relatively low and it is tempting to spread the cost of making components over several models that otherwise compete strongly in the market place. Indeed such common sourcing has become commonplace, and many of the most respected modern rivals produce vehicles which comprise almost standard assemblies of proprietary engines, and transmissions, and axles. Some indeed have never made any of these units for themselves.

Many of the commercial vehicle manufacturers which ultimately became part of the British Leyland Motor Corporation had for much of their separate existences produced most of their own major sub-assemblies. The qualifications are necessary for few of them had their own foundries and therefore bought in unmachined castings and forgings. Hardly any made their own electrical equipment, after the earliest years at any rate, and while several had at one time or another body building shops none, of course, made rubber tyres or glass. Moreover there were times when home produced units were not available, or suitable, or to the customer's taste, and other items had to be substituted. The cost of research and development grew enormously with the passing of time and inevitably the dependence on outside suppliers grew: now the lineal descendants of the companies that form the modern Leyland also use quantities of proprietary engines and transmissions. Not that this circumstance is altogether new: in earlier – much earlier – times a common design of boiler was used by the joint founders of Leyland itself, Coulthard and Lancashire Steam Motor.

In view of the sad fact that its ultimate demise was due at least in part to being over-fond of its own not very good engines, it is a little ironic that Crossley made the power units for some early Leylands, and also for a number of Halleys. These were petrol engines of course, but when Crossley took up the diesel cause not only did it produce the first all-British diesel bus, a double decker, but its products were used – briefly – by Scammell, Albion, and Associated Daimler, among others. And a considerable number of older chassis were also re-engined with Crossley units, some Leylands among them. The debt was duly repaid: convenient and satisfactory replacements for the engines in post-1945 Crossley chassis were found to be Leyland diesels.

Halley was in many ways an unlucky company and has long since been sunk in oblivion. It began as the Glasgow Motor Lorry Company in workshops vacated by Albion and, in addition to using Crossley engines, bought some from Tylor, which supplied AEC for many years. Quite soon Halley moved to new premises but by 1935 the sands had run out; Albion took over, largely because of those excellent workshops. Other factors were in play, but Halley too had made the mistake of spending much time and money on an engine that would not come right. There was also a more substantial link with AEC: during the First World War AEC was turning out three- and four-tonner lorries by the hundred, and Halley manufactured parts for them.

Tylor engines were used by several firms but only AEC, blaming the government, apologised for their performance. That was in the thousands of lorries made to military specifications during the First World War, when AEC engine production facilities were unable to meet the demand, and the disclaimer no doubt reflected company concern for its post-war reputation. As it happened the firm was already deeply involved in sharing another power unit, for as a result of some complicated negotiations it had, from 1913 to 1916, been making chassis which were sold on the open market as Daimlers. Many of these had Daimler engines but not all, and an appreciable

number of all-AEC vehicles entered service with Daimler cast in to their radiator top tanks.

In part this paid back an otherwise unacknowledged debt to Daimler, for the founder of the AEC line of buses was admitted by its designer to be an amalgam of other designs, and said by its detractors to be nothing more than a Daimler-Wolseley-Straker. AEC and Daimler lived on in the bus business, Wolseley moved to other things, and Straker died without issue in the mid-1920s.

The London General Omnibus Company, parent of AEC, did not abandon all its own constructional ambitions. From time to time over the following twenty years it built buses of its own design from the wheels up, and bodied thousands more. There was even a sizeable batch of light vans produced at the General's Chiswick overhaul works. That was during 1924, in which year the LGOC began a programme of assembling several hundred AECs for its own use. Later a batch of Chiswick-made single deckers were fitted with Daimler sleeve valve power units, and a handful of experimental buses made during the end of this period originally had Meadows engines, later exchanged for AEC.

There was to be another period, at the end of the 1920s, when AEC operated a joint company with Daimler, and again AEC built the vehicles and Daimler some of the engines. The trading name this time was Associated Daimler and the partnership soon ended, largely because the latter was wedded to an expensive and complicated sleeve valve petrol engine while the former was moving rapidly forward with a brand new range of chassis all its own, and also into diesel engines. When, following the break, Daimler began in earnest to make its own complete chassis again both petrol and diesel engines were offered. Soon, in order to increase market appeal, the universally accepted Gardner engines had to be included in Daimler sales brochures – in which, it has to be said, the company was not alone, but it is worth remarking that Guy found that in its larger passenger vehicles the Daimler sleeve valve engine was a selling aid, if not for long. The last significant adventure in diesel engine development by Daimler was the joint manufacturing agreement for a high speed V6

The driver's workplace, hitherto given scant regard, began to exercise an increasing effect on buying decisions, particularly after the first European premium trucks began to arrive in Britain. AEC, never having had a bodybuilding department of its own, had traditionally left it to distributors and customers to make provision for cabs, issuing sets of recommended drawings so that not only were the resulting structures acceptable from the engineering point of view but would also have a family likeness. After Park Royal joined AEC its influence naturally spread into cab making, but as these three examples from around 1960 show there were still considerable differences, from a half-cab (**below**) for a special customer, by way of divided – and opening – windscreen with narrow doors (**left**), to wraparound screen with wide doors (**below left**).

EV 2769
SEBASTIAN
Daimler

Left: This long-lived Daimler tower wagon, working in New Zealand, was one of the flitched timber chassised subvention designs which owed much to AEC collaboration.

Top: Until recent times the standard Leyland chassis for heavy overseas work in oil-fields and the like were typified by this vintage-looking Super Hippo.

Above: Guy persevered long after the others in building 'premium' lightweights. But before the 1950s were out the battle had been lost to the mass-producers.

designed by Cummins. But that was right at the end of Daimler's separate existence.

Throughout the petrol era Guy had little difficulty in producing acceptable engines of its own, but prudently the company decided to rely on specialist suppliers for its diesels. Gardner, not destined to become part of Leyland, was for long a favourite, backed up by Meadows – which had also made a steady trickle of petrol engines for Guy. The steady decline in Guy fortunes before the company changed hands and its rise again afterwards were marked by its almost total dependence on outside suppliers and abandonment of own-sourcing. Leyland, BMC, and especially AEC all delivered large consignments of parts to the Guy factory, and some of the Guy heavy chassis of the 1950s comprised mainly AEC components: a prototype of the ill-starred Wulfrunian bus was Leyland-powered.

For so long as petrol reigned supreme Scammell was almost entirely self-sufficient in unit sourcing, but it had the good sense to recognise that oil engines were something else, and henceforward relied on specialists. Gardner was to become a long-standing favourite, as with so many others, but almost every other make of suitable engine has at some time been fitted to a Scammell, including Meadows, Albion, and AEC from the long rank of companies which ultimately became British Leyland. With component rationalisation schemes during its ownership by Leyland, Scammell products were produced with Leyland engines, Albion drive axles, and gearboxes made by either Self Changing Gears, another group company, or by the old Thornycroft plant to AEC designs.

For many years spare engine making capacity

among a few of the large volume chassis producers caused them to seek sales outside and to become serious competitors for the specialist power unit suppliers. On the home market alone Bristol added Leyland engines to the Gardners it bought for lorries it made during the 1950s, although Leyland had no direct interest in the firm until 1965. And one of the few indications of a shortlived shareholding during the 1960s by Leyland in Fodens was the use of engines by the former in addition to the products of Gardner and its own factory by the latter. In fact it was a trade at which Leyland showed considerable aptitude: Bedford bought many Leyland engines; Heathfield used them in dump trucks; Seddon installed them in a successful range of heavy lorries; and many owners of chassis made in rival factories found Leyland engines satisfactory substitutes for whatever power units had previously been fitted.

Seddon also used Gardner of course — and AEC, for in this line of business as in so many others the two giants competed fiercely. The insignificant British Mack during its short existence offered both makes (sometimes using Albion gearboxes too) and so did the equally shortlived Rowe, which also added Meadows to the choice. MTN, otherwise Rutland, and one of the more successful young hopefuls of the post-1945 era, occasionally used Leyland or Meadows engines instead of its standard Gardners or Perkins, and Dodge in Britain, while still American-owned, fitted Leyland and AEC power units in addition to its staple Perkins, and also added BMC gearboxes in some models.

Links were even stronger with Douglas, by far the longest survivor of the post-war boom in new motor manufacturers, for this firm began by lightly

Far left column: The solution to many of Leyland Motors cab problems came in 1964, for the Ergomatic cab was well up to the standards of its day and capable of being adapted to almost any chassis within its range. It was capable of being tilted, thereby catching up with what had been standard American practice for years, and also permitted ready access to engines and other front-end components. The Ergomatic provided one of the earliest tangible signs of unity within LMC, for it quickly replaced Park Royal and other cabs on otherwise largely unchanged chassis, and, made in thinner gauge steel, was also fitted to Albions. **Top to bottom:** The Luton-headed Mercury van illustrates one difficulty with tilt cabs – the need to provide removable parts of the vehicle body; the Super Reiver shows how perfunctory were the efforts to provide a distinct identity for the old marques; the Octopus was fitted with filler panels that raised the cab; while the Marathon has the same structure mounted high, and with a sleeper extension added.

Scammell contrived to preserve, in the matter of cabs, much of the individuality that it kept elsewhere. The four by four Mountaineer of 1950 (**top centre**) for oilfield and similar work has a cab much of which was inherited from Bedford, and which saw considerable use elsewhere in the Scammell range of vehicles. The rear-steering Trunker (**above**) is fitted with the moulded plastics cab designed by Italian car stylist Michelotti (who worked also for Triumph) and used throughout the 1960s and 1970s on most of Scammell's haulage machines. Samson (**left**), the eight by four tractor for 75 tons gross loads, of which a few were made around 1970, has a version of the Motor Panels cab used on Crusader, and also on the Guy Big J, among several others.

Several Australian cities once relied upon double-decked buses, and although generally of British appearance they were distinctive. AEC supplied many; this is a Regal IV in Sydney.

3R0
JENHAM ST BONDI

Above: Every so often there comes into prominence an operator, bus or lorry, who decides to build a model of its own. Such a one was the Cornish coach company which, through the 1950s, produced a great many designs for goods and passenger work under the name Rowe Hillmaster. The lorries had relatively conventional chassis and so, too, by 1955, had this underfloor-engined bus. The power unit was a four-cylinder Meadows diesel, transmitting through a Meadows gearbox. Few were made, for Rowe concentrated on its lorries in which a choice of Meadows, Leyland, or AEC power units might be fitted. Meadows, next door neighbour to Guy in Wolverhampton, joined Jaguar in the mid-1960s. Now no trace remains.

Above right: In its earliest years Scammell had been self-sufficient, and indeed it remained largely so even after its adoption of proprietary diesel engines. But one of the advantages to be derived from the merger with Leyland Motors was access to a wide range of components: quite soon axles from Albion, AEC gearboxes from Thornycroft, and semi-automatic transmissions from Self Changing Gears were being used – with, of course, some group cabs. This Handyman of 1960 has a Leyland engine but the rest is Scammell – gate-change gearbox, double reduction epicyclic rear axle, and all. Equally Scammell is the rubber suspended semi-trailer, fitted with the company's own heavy duty automatic coupling.

modifying ex-military AEC Matadors and went on to transform Leyland Comets. In addition many products and components from other companies were modified or used by Douglas in building an enormous variety of vehicles, and sometimes the results were powered by Leyland or Meadows, and included SCG transmissions. In the main Coventry Climax (ultimately to find refuge in Jaguar) made engines for passenger cars rather than heavy commercial vehicles, but a large Lycoming unit it made under licence from the American factory during the 1920s and 1930s was supplied to the long-dead Gilford company alongside Meadows and Leyland units. Also during the 1930s Meadows was on the list of suppliers to independent chassis builder Garner, which used Austin as well, and many years later the Jensen company used Austin power units for its little Jen-Tug, which it was hoped might come to rival the Scammell Mechanical Horse. Crane maker Hydrocon used reinforced but otherwise standard Albion chassis for its lorry-mounted cranes.

Dennis was once a self-sufficient concern which progressed by degrees into becoming an assembler and at stages in its career has used engines by AEC, BMC, and even Jaguar, among others. AWD (All Wheel Drive) and Coles favoured

AEC engines for their special purpose crane carriers, and in a distinctly uncharacteristic transformation much of an AEC Monarch was converted in 1938 into a battery-electric refuse collector by Shefflex. In another electrical byway of the 1930s, Harrods, the world-famous London department store, built for itself a sizeable fleet of battery-powered delivery vans which used Morris-Commercial running gear. There were other collaborations in producing complete vehicles; one of the last deliveries of peacetime buses in 1939-40 was a large batch of chassisless trolley buses built by MCW, with AEC components. During the post-1945 new vehicles famine, bodybuilders John Beadle produced an integral coach body that could be fitted with major components of several makes and AEC, Leyland, and Morris units were often used. A more determined effort along the same lines produced the chassisless Leyland-MCW Olympic buses of the 1950s.

One of the characteristic features of the massproduced American-style light and medium weight lorries which became so popular from the 1930s on was their comfortable cabs, which usually bore a considerable resemblance in construction and trim to cars made by the same companies. Gradually other commercial vehicles

Left: In its heyday Park Royal, which had arisen from the remains of Hall Lewis, an earlier bodybuilder, was wholeheartedly willing to collaborate with other firms which might have been considered rivals. Among them was Guy, in the post-1945 era becoming uneasily aware that sheer size was going to be increasingly important in the struggle for survival. So, reasoned Guy, if it could again offer modern bodywork on bus chassis, then a competitive edge could be gained. The company turned to Park Royal, which supplied substantially complete frames to which Guy added some panelling, the trim, seats, and finishing. This Meadows-engined sample was completed in 1949.

One of the earliest successful builders of chassisless
buses and coaches in
Britain was John C. Beadle,
and for a decade or so after
1945 built many vehicles.
Into some were installed
new engines, transmissions
and running gear but a large
number used mechanical
units salvaged from
scrapped buses, usually
double deckers whose own
bodies had gone beyond
economic repair. Leyland
and AEC, as in this example,
were the usual donors. No
attempt was made to re-
engineer the secondhand
components and so it was
not possible to incorporate a
front overhang and forward
entrance. Nevertheless, the
vehicles were handsome
enough and lasted well.

From its earliest days the
Northern General Transport
concern enjoyed making
some of its own buses. Usually AEC components were
used and among the more
startling creations of NGT
was a sizable fleet of six-
wheeled buses and coaches
which took the side-engined
AEC Q theme into new
realms of capacity and comfort. A later batch were actually assembled by AEC. This
1933 picture (**left**) shows how
the American-origin power
units of the first delivery
allowed a nearly flat floor –
lacking in the Q. More than
20 years later came
conventional-looking single
deckers with 'home-made'
chassis (**above and below**),
which by careful rearranging, squeezed in several
more seats than their Regal
cousins could manage.

15 A TOWN CENTRE
BRICKWOODS BEERS
Ta ste the sun go down
HCR 136D

Guy became a powerful competitor in the post-1945 double and single-decked bus market, but gradually demand moved away from its traditionally styled designs.

Opposite top left: Probably the greatest failing of the post-1945 Crossley diesel engines was lack of development, for their short-comings, notably poor fuel economy and overheating, should have been curable. Matters were not helped by company weakness for inefficient fluid trans-missions – and there had been a pre-1939 history of unreliability too. But during the famine years of the late 1940s operators would buy almost anything, including Crossleys; the transmis-sions were usually the first item to be replaced, by con-ventional gearboxes, and many vehicles also lost their Crossley engines. The Ley-land 8·6-litre unit was found to fit nicely. Later, some Crossley gearboxes were fitted to AECs.

By the end of the 1960s the number of Leyland engine users in Europe alone was impressive, and the com-pany could claim as regular customers: DAF and Verheul in The Netherlands; the Danish DAB; Brossel, of Bel-gium; Sisu in Finland; and OAF in Austria. In eastern Europe both Ikarus (Hun-gary) and ITV (Yugoslavia) took Leyland group pro-ducts, and in France Wil-leme, Vernay, and Berliet. The Spanish Pegaso and Italian OMT were on the list, too. Sisu, in which Leyland then held a minority interest, was a big customer over many years, and this snow plough of 1965 took one of a batch of 660 power units. By then the grand total supplied had reached more than 9,000 engines.

makers found themselves having to face the fact that good though their chassis may be, the cabs left a great deal to be desired. The difficulty, once again, was largely a matter of initial manufac-turing cost balanced against the number of cabs required; it is simply not possible to make high quality units at a low enough price. Indeed, nowadays it is generally recognised that the cost of tooling up for a new cab is almost prohibitive, which explains why designs from all makers have such long and largely unchanged lives.

This intractable problem has given rise to some curious results. There was, during the 1960s, a distinctively bulbous cab made jointly for Leyland, Albion – and Dodge. Scammell tried a version of it too. Earlier, the bonneted Leyland Comet had also shared pressings with a Dodge, and when Bed-ford finally abandoned the cab which adorned thousands of its neat little goods chassis during the 1940s and 1950s Scammell took it up with pleasure, and grafted it on to some of its biggest regular products. Another unit elegantly styled with lightweight vehicles in mind was the pretty cab structure used not only on Guy Otters and Thornycroft Tridents, but also on the largest chassis to leave the Thornycroft works, not to mention an occasional AEC and even Dodge. One of the most remarkable multiple user successes was the set of proprietary cab panels and parts which were to a greater or lesser degree applied by Guy, Scammell, and about a dozen others from all over Europe. But perhaps the oddest outcome of Leyland group rationalisation turned Scammell and Standard Triumph into joint users of the pressed steel cab normally fitted to a 15-20 cwt Standard panel van. Scammell used it on a not very successful four-wheeled version of the Scarab urban tractor.

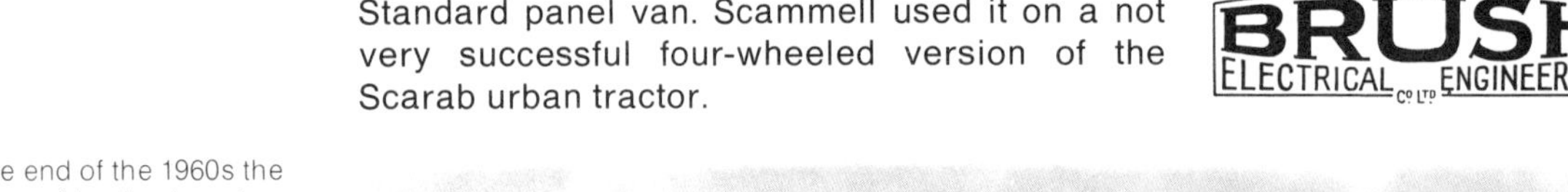

By the mid-1950s vehicle cabs were assuming a greater importance than ever before, and they were becoming much more expensive to make. Expediency forced upon several of the smaller firms the decision to share designs, and therefore production costs, with others. This elegant proprietary cab (**below**) was much used by Guy for its smaller models and also by Thornycroft for a family of lightweight chassis. Surprisingly it was also perched on some of the largest Thornycrofts, including this Big Ben dumper (**above right**), where it could look rather odd. The Leyland (**above**) is a curiosity. High production figures meant that home (and most overseas) Leylands almost invariably carried company cabs.

POST OFFICE
INTERNATIONAL
TELEGRAPH
SERVICES

TELEGRAPH MANAGER,
ELECTRA HOUSE,
VICTORIA EMBANKMENT,
LONDON, W.C.2

The Post Office was the largest individual buyer of the LD van, and of its successor, the EA. But this LD is in the later colours of Post Office Telephones and was operated by PO International Telegraph Services.

Trucks

Opposite top: Early Leyland motor vehicles, like those of virtually every other bus and lorry maker, had their engines at the front where they could be easily reached for the daily, almost hourly, attention they required. But chassis had necessarily to be long in relation to payloads. In order to produce a vehicle better suited to narrower streets, Leyland, in 1906, produced its X-type, which sacrificed accessibility to convenience by placing the driving position high above the engine. The model proved popular with dockside hauliers, and particularly municipal service fleets, and as this 1913 version shows for a 5-tonner it really was quite compact.

One of the more remarkable aspects of early lorry history is that long journeys were regularly undertaken almost from the beginning. Overseas markets where, probably, railway links were sparse became natural forcing grounds for mechanical road transport; much more surprising was the rate at which the trend grew in Britain, which by 1900 had an excess of rail routes and services.

Of course, it has to be said that all things are relative. 'Heavy' lorries in 1901 meant payloads in the region of four tons; 'long' journeys were hardly more than 30 or 40 miles. However, although with legal speeds in the region of 5 mph they seemed long enough and the handful of vehicles actually making such expeditions was tiny, it still comprised a sizeable proportion of the total number in use. But they were hardly a threat to the railway companies.

Another reason why railwaymen continued to sleep soundly in their beds was the kind of work that motor transport generally was opening up for itself. Perhaps it was loyalty to a then local manufacturer that persuaded the Chiswick local authority in London in 1898 to buy Thornycroft steam waggons for its transport needs; it was not long, at any rate, before Westminster City Council bought Leylands for similar work. Flour mills were early enthusiasts for heavy motors: their cargoes were weighty, sold in large quantities, and delivery was usually required to local high streets and corner shops. It was a pattern of demand well suited to steam waggons and trailers, and one that Fowler, Aveling, Clayton, and others were eager to supply.

By the outbreak of war in 1914 virtually all experimenting in basic vehicle design was over and the definitive form of heavy lorry had evolved, to be adopted by nearly every maker. A major influence for every British manufacturer was the subvention scheme, a clever government plan which gave the armed forces access to thousands of privately-owned vehicles. Their civilian owners received an annual cash payment, the subvention, for each one, promising in return to make it available in times of national emergency. In order to become eligible the vehicles had to conform to a broad specification that was aimed at easing hitherto major problems of crew and maintenance familiarisation; wheel and tyre interchangeability; and also bodywork and equipment fittings.

The first subvention specification was published in 1912, and it had the effect of concentrating the thoughts of manufacturers and users on series of straightforward chassis – three-tonners to the army, which would be four, five, and even six-tonners to civilian hauliers who had to make a living. These vehicles closely approximated to the AEC B-type bus of 1910 in their general configuration and therefore had large understressed four-cylinder petrol engines at the front with the driving positions behind them. The transmission had to be 'live' – that is, with a propeller shaft driving a rear axle containing the differential gear. Chain drive was not permitted.

So successful were these sturdy machines that not only did they, in their thousands, keep the British war effort on the move, but later they also supplied much of the rapidly burgeoning transport required for the brave new post-war world. Indeed, it took profound changes in legislation to finally drive them into the scrapyards, and a few lingered on in everyday service through the 1930s, 1940s, and even (just) into the 1950s.

Those legislative changes of the early 1930s had the primary purpose of redefining the role of road transport which, it was envisaged, would play a secondary role to railways. But it was the more or less simultaneous perfecting of giant pneumatic tyres which had the more profound effect on commercial vehicle development. This new shock absorbing tyre equipment made possible high speed running, and chassis no longer

Steam waggons usually came in either of two sorts – overtypes, like the Clayton opposite, and undertypes. This 1906 model by the Lancashire Steam Motor Company shows clearly how the latter got its name. Placing the engine under the floor in this way distributed its weight evenly over the axles, and shortened drive arrangements to the rear wheels. It was, however, much exposed to road dirt, and was not under the eye of the crew. A bigger drawback was the boiler: most undertypes, including this one, had vertical boilers, which could not be large enough to hold great reserves while also being sensitive to fuel and firing methods.

needed to be so solidly constructed as they had been in the old bone jarring, bolt loosening, days. It followed that engines must also be made lighter and faster, with transmissions to match.

Nearly every maker rose to the occasion and produced chassis well able to meet new challenges. Indeed on reflection it is remarkable how few companies failed to design and produce, in a very short space of time, thoroughly modern and generally acceptable vehicles, particularly when it is borne in mind that 1930-31 lay in the middle of a terrible world slump in trade, and that several of those same firms were also in the throes of producing their own first series of diesel engines. Certainly it makes a thought-provoking contrast to events twenty or so years later, when those same chassis designs reached their final limits of development and became due in their turn for total replacement. Fewer makers then felt the effort would be worthwhile.

Among many detailed provisions of the 1933 changes in British traffic law were strictly enforceable axle and gross weight limits and higher speeds for lighter vehicles. This combination virtually eradicated what was left of an already very sick steam waggon business. It also formed an ideal seedbed for the new high speed diesel engines, and generally helped to bring British heavy vehicle makers into line with western Europe and America. But not for long: those speed and weight limits, reasonable by the standards of the early 1930s, were to endure for too many years and thereby seriously hamper development.

In fairness, so did the Second World War, with the result that when production for civilian use got under way again in 1946 heavy vehicles in particular bore a marked resemblance to their 1930s forebears. And post-war conditions were such that the same could be said of too many products of the 1950s, too.

This lack of progress was causing mischief. Before the war a case could be made for regarding railways as the dominant form of land transport, and from force of habit as much as anything this attitude persisted until the early 1950s. By then it was seriously hampering econo-

mic growth at home and, apart from Commonwealth markets, export sales of vehicles too. When finally government was forced to permit the next stage in road transport development it was too late for all but the most determined survivors – which, among the companies that were ultimately to shelter under the Leyland banner, meant Leyland itself followed at an increasing distance by AEC.

Although the self-evident step of increasing payload capacity by adding another axle to a four-wheeler had occurred to many people during the 1920s – not least to steam waggon makers, who faced singularly difficult tare weight to payload ratio problems – it was the strictly limited tolerance to overloads of the pneumatic tyre that persuaded manufacturers to start really thinking about multi-axle chassis for goods carrying. Tyre capacity coupled, that is, with a clear resolution on the part of authority to enforce vehicle weight limits in the future.

Users had already found that it was no simple matter of just slinging another axle under the frame; all too often in fact they did just that and while the result might be tolerated with the low speeds and generally primitive conditions of the 1920s, times were rapidly changing. By 1930 there were two distinct approaches to the

Below: Many advantages were claimed for overtype steam waggons but, as these Claytons of 1918 show, economy of road space and cab visibility were not among them. Nor, all too often, was driver comfort. But overtypes, which had their engines on top of the locomotive-type boilers, were rugged and simple machines, well suited to the abuse suffered by all early heavy goods vehicles. Clayton Wagons, earlier Clayton and Shuttleworth, had entered the waggon business in 1912, and it was an extension of a large general and agricultural engineering business. Like many another, similar, concern the First World War exhausted it and the 1920s gave no opportunity to recover. The remains of Clayton were acquired by Marshall in 1930.

Right: An enduring success
overseas is the Ashok Leyland India concern, which
takes standard products but
produces much of them
locally – including cabs.

Below: Oil companies have
been big users of what
became Leyland Group
chassis for many years.
Shellmex and BP was the
user of the Albion and AEC
tankers pictured and also
ran Scammells from the
same depot.

Opposite: AEC depended on
outside firms to provide its
lorry cabs, and many of
these last generation
chassis had good-looking
cabs built by associates
Park Royal.

FINE FARE
FINE FARE
BRITAIN'S LEADING SUPERMARKETS
8561 RO
90

The tale of the First World War RAF Leylands is part of transport folklore: how the company bought back more than 4,000 war worn vehicles and set up a factory to recondition them. Less well known is that financially the whole escapade almost ruined the firm. But the rebuilds were good machines. The original specification was sound, and in the end most RAF Leylands were scrapped through obsolescence rather than wear. The victory parade sample with a Sopwith fighter on board (**right**) is typical of the breed in service trim. Maple may have been the last user of licensed RAF Leylands: this one (**far right**) was still running in 1952.

Even the passing of 35 years is not the whole explanation of the progress from the Morris cab of 1924 and its BMC successor of 1959. A prime difference is in the manufacturing methods: Morris output, even of the best-selling one-tonner, was not great enough to justify anything more elaborate than a simple wooden framing with flat sheet panels (**below left**). BMC could expect continuing production runs of many thousands, making car-type press tooling and assembly possible (**below right**). Then, of course, driver expectations increased out of all measure. While the Morris provided an undoubted improvement on the horse carter's lot, drivers now expect car levels of comfort.

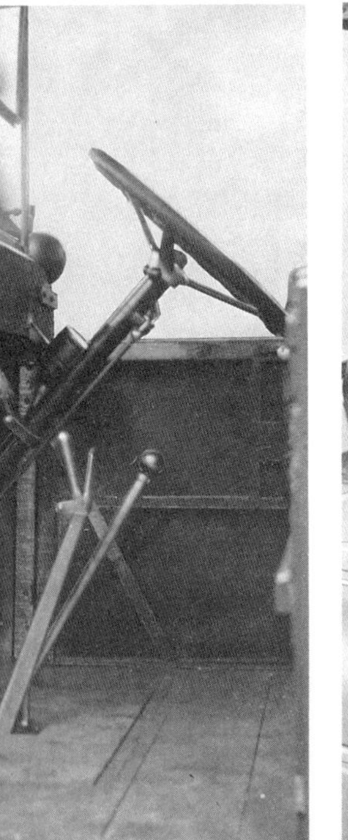

Leyland Motors was not the only maker of subsidy chassis used in the First World War: every other factory of any importance also produced suitable machines. The scheme was simple – owners received regular payments from government on the understanding that vehicles would be handed over during national emergencies. The technical specifications created motors that had uniform control layouts and body dimensions, and were generally similar in appearance and performance. The Thornycroft mobile workshops (**centre left**), drawn 'somewhere in France' during 1918, show one version; Wolseley built some with armoured bodywork (**below**), front row, in addition to lorries, back; and Maudslays were as welcome as other survivors in post-war haulage (**left**).

Recabbing in modern style
did remarkable things to the
appearance of a pre-1940
Leyland Beaver. Such
changes are rare: few goods
chassis outlive their
bodywork.

H & R. AINSCOUGH LTD
LEYLAND
18
18
H & R. AINSCOUGH LTD
FLOUR MILLERS.
GRAIN MERCHANTS
BURSCOUGH
BURSCOUGH 3131
GTD 1

Left: Part of the Albion contribution to the British war effort during the years from 1939 to 1945 was a large number of these heavy gun tractors. They had a nominal capacity of 10 tons and where possible incorporated components used in civilian vehicles. An interesting reflection on the possible spheres of operation are the double-skinned tropical roof to the cab, and a radiator muff. Albion was a steady if unobtrusive supplier of military vehicles; more generally favoured were – and are – those manufacturers with production capacities large enough to take on the usually specialised designs needed, without affecting outputs of regular models for ordinary use.

Below: The British postal authorities saw some worthwhile publicity might result from mobile post offices, and so took into service three articulateds for use at county shows and the like. For them were obtained the perfect registration numbers – GPO 1, GPO 2, and GPO 3. The tractors were Morris-Commercial Leaders of the type introduced during the mid-1930s and in articulated form had a rated capacity of about 6 tons. The General Post Office were for many years loyal supporters of Morris and Morris-Commercial, and apart from buying many thousands of standard vehicles also commissioned many specials designed to meet its own requirements.

problems and opportunities of six-wheelers. One was the purpose-designed articulated pioneered by Scammell in 1922 and soon enthusiastically imitated by others, notably AEC and Leyland. The second comprised an updated and properly designed rigid load-carrying chassis with two axles at the back and one at the front. This familiar-sounding arrangement was found, however, to conceal a number of complications.

There was the question of how many tyres, for a start. Four-wheelers on solids almost invariably had twins on the rear wheels in order to share out the load and to provide adequate grip in what were often muddy and slimy conditions. On pneumatics the first consideration certainly still held, although the second did not. But careful calculation showed that sufficient extra carrying capacity could be gained by adding a simple trailing axle mounted on single tyres. Maudslay had sold some solid-tyred lorries thus arranged and then some more on pneumatics; AEC and others tried it too, but owners found the problems of weight disposition too limiting. There was a brief revival in the 1960s, though, when for a short while something might be gained by adding a single-tyred self-steering axle to an otherwise standard and probably lightweight four-wheeled chassis.

By definition, dividing the imposed load over four wheels instead of two will halve the available grip on ground surfaces and while operators on smooth roads are not much inconvenienced by this, off-road running on building sites and the like can soon induce wheel-spinning frustration. Double drive was clearly the answer – except that new problems were induced by the two drive axles 'fighting' each other when negotiating corners. The solution to that was a third differential gear, fitted between drive axles so that, in combination with those already part of the axles, it would equalise the driving effort between all four wheels. With the further need for compensating suspensions to keep all four rear wheels pressed equally on the road, it all became both weighty and complicated and, indeed, remains so still.

Inevitably, once the finer details of the new

legislation had been fully digested, the rigid six idea was taken further to become the rigid eight, and from the mid-1930s onward for three decades nearly every heavy vehicle factory made them. They became the archetypal long distance lorry in Britain, often hauling drawbar trailers behind them. Having evolved the rigid eight, it followed that someone would, in effect, remove a drive axle from it and produce a twin-steering six-wheeler which would combine high carrying capacity with low unladen weight while, at the same time, be much more manoeuvrable than conventional three-axled machines. The first of their kind appeared just before war broke out in 1939 and although the type has never really thrived, it is still made in small numbers.

But the great success story among multi-axled lorries is the articulated.

Its origins can be taken back to the point at which the first steerable horse-drawn waggon was built, but a more realistic starting point is a Thornycroft entered for the 1898 Liverpool self-

READY MIXED CONCRETE LTD
61350
61350
LEYLAND
VRK 910G

Opposite: Over many years Leyland has had considerable success with chassis modified for use as concrete mixers. This one was providing material to help strengthen the roof of the London District Underground tunnels.

Above: Last of the Scammell-built urban tractors in the Mechanical Horse idiom was the Townsman. Automatic couplings permitted rapid interchanging of semi-trailers.

Left: One of the most successful low-level 'delivery' cabs was made by Albion for Leyland. However, although the need for the special cab was real, demand was not strong for this variant.

Manufacture of the 30 m.p.h. Lynx is now well under way. Here is an illustration of one of the early orders just completed. Weighing, unladen, under 50 cwt., it is designed for pay-loads of 6 tons.
May we send you particulars?

Leyland Motors
– Ltd –

HEAD OFFICE & WORKS   LEYLAND · LANCS

Above: It was the Regal-Regent family of buses which gave AEC the base on which to build a worthwhile lorry business. Lorries had indeed been made for years, but the tribe of Mercurys, Monarchs, and Mammoths introduced from 1930 onwards was a turning point. A great help, of course, was the availability of a bus-proved diesel engine, one of the first reliable units of its kind. This Mammoth is carrying an early transit concrete mixer, a class of machine not much in demand while labour was cheap and willing. But the 1930s saw also an increasing trend toward mass-concrete construction, a trend that has continued – together with transit mixers.

Below: Despite its discouraging experiences with heavy vehicles Morris-Commercial persevered with medium weights – and achieved considerable successes. From the late 1930s until the merger with Austin the Equiload range reigned, with this 5-tonner as the largest. The uncommon semi-forward control cab had several advantages: as the model name implies, imposed weight could be shared more evenly between front and rear axles but, unlike full forward control, there was more space in the cab (it seated three), and access to the engine was marginally improved. The latter consideration waned as the servicing requirements of power units lessened.

The operational advantages of conventional rigid six-wheeled lorries were plain: carrying capacity could be increased both practically and legally. But there were drawbacks, of which the most significant were more tyres to wear. And for some kinds of cargoes the sole front axle could easily become overloaded. Twin-steer (**below**), colloquially the Chinese Six, overcame these problems, and improved directional stability into the bargain. Albion began making them in 1939 and, much later, BMC-BLMC-Leyland Vehicles products were among the lighter chassis converted for use in the drinks trade (**right**); an attraction was the use of small wheels and low deck.

propelled lorry trials. This vehicle was clearly a self-contained tractor unit, on the rear of which was supported the front end of a load-carrying semi-trailer. The two parts of the vehicle were joined by a flexible coupling that permitted the combination to negotiate horizontal and vertical curves, and some of the semi-trailer deadweight and its payload, were borne by the tractor. This was to become the essential definition of an articulated lorry, and many subsequent attempts to improve upon it, usually by means of complicated and heavy devices intended to combine rigid and flexible chassis, or semi- and full drawbar trailers, have usually failed.

The real beginning of recognisably modern articulation came in 1920 from the old-established London firm G. Scammell and Nephew, then, and for years afterwards, coach builders, wheelwrights, and steam waggon repairers. One of the family saw some primitive tractor-trailer combinations of American make and realised the potential. Careful design and the wise adoption of internal combustion produced a vehicle that was an instant technical and commercial success. Scammell Lorries Ltd was therefore established

to exploit this new kind of vehicle – but British law at that time imposed stringent weight and speed limitations upon vehicles drawing trailers, and so the Scammell was officially a flexible six-wheeler, with its semi-trailer always described as a carrier.

Scammell became artists in articulation, and while rapid development was possible always left its rivals far behind. Its *pièce de résistance* was certainly the first 100-tonner in the world, but of longer lasting significance was its work on chassisless tanker semi-trailers. Another Scammell articulated designed, like the first, to exploit a legislative loophole was the Mechanical Horse – although in this case the essential design was purchased from aero engine makers Napier. With the Mechanical Horse, foaled by a quirk of law and eventually to be put down by another, came the automatic coupling for semi-trailers, a device which made it practicable for one Horse to service three load carriers: one loading, one unloading, and one in transit.

Articulation rapidly gained in popularity during what remained of the solid-tyred era, but really came into its own with the advent of limited capacity pneumatics. For a while articulation, like rigid six-wheelers, reached absurd limits with the most unlikely chassis being used as tractors. Soon, however, the initial exuberance wore off leaving tribes of models, many of which were decidedly flimsy. For years limitations on gross weights were such that most articulated lorries were bought either because of their great manoeuvrability in confined spaces, or for reasons of low first cost. A lightly constructed tractor unit, probably mass-produced, coupled to an unsophisticated semi-trailer of the time, could do the work of a much more robust 'premium' six or eight-wheeler – and for a fraction of the outlay. Total life costs were probably another matter.

But when during the mid-1960s legislation changed again it was to heavily bias matters in favour of articulation, and British factories raced to reach standards of vehicle size and stamina that had been the norm in America and elsewhere for decades. This was the crucial point at which the present flow of imported vehicles into British road transport began and despite sterling efforts by the modern Leyland factories, coupled with more recent easings of legislative requirements, it will not be easy to turn back the tide of imports.

Opposite top left and bottom: The political under and overtones surrounding Bristol during its days in state ownership created an unnatural and on the whole undesirable climate in heavy vehicle manufacture. Restricting the company to supplying only bus operators within the state fleet removed pricing competition and when in 1952, after an absence of more than 20 years, it re-entered the lorry business it did so at the expense of privately-funded manufacturers, even though sales were again restricted to sister companies. In their day, the Bristol lorries were straightforward machines, typifying conventional thought. Production ceased when new designs were needed to meet increased gross weight limits.

Opposite top right: Within the truly enormous Thornycroft range of the 1930s could be found a model to meet every commercial need, although many of the individual designs, on close examination, would be seen to comprise relatively few standardised components. The Trusty was a lightweight for 7 to 8 ton loads and it was aimed at operators needing to combine quite-large capacity with the ability to negotiate narrow docksides, railway sidings, and crowded streets. The set-back front axle, long a Thornycroft hallmark, reduced turning circles and also helped to share weight more evenly. This Trusty was in use during the Second World War, hence the white-edged wings.

The Boxer was one of a doggy family (Mastiff, Boxer, Terrier) of revisions introduced by BLMC as updated versions of Bathgate-built BMC vehicles. In their new form the heavier ones would have been directly competitive with ex-Albion products and so the two ranges were effectively merged, being sold for a time as Leyland Redline. The all-important cab was also ex-BMC, but heavily reworked for its new role. The Boxer, in addition to selling quite well for ordinary haulage purposes, also proved to be suitable for municipal work and an appreciable number went in to this specialised application. The roadsweeper (**top**), like many of its kind, has twin driving positions; the refuse collector (**above**) has a load-compressing moving bulkhead in the body.

Buses

Old style composite body-work, with metal panelling on wooden frames had obvious limitations of inherent strength and resistance to loadings. All-metal (or nearly so) construction allowed structures in which the strength of each component could be accurately calculated (**below**), thereby reducing unnecessary weight and producing a more efficient vehicle. Leyland Motors, during the late 1930s, was building fleets of trolley buses for London and hit on this scheme (**bottom**) for demonstrating the strength of their steel framing. A full load of 77 men were installed – and the body sagged just 0.625 in. That was without the external panelling, which would add some stiffness, or a chassis either.

Notwithstanding their large and uncompromising natures buses proved to be insubstantial product lines for a great many makers of commercial vehicles. Difficulties lay not so much in the engineering, although the peculiarly troublesome operating conditions in urban bus work caught unawares several makers who should have had no difficulty in producing suitably durable machinery, but rather more from the need to attract and hold large enough sales.

A great deal of money and effort was, and is, needed to develop a bus capable of doing everything required of it, and at acceptable cost of ownership. Unless enough sales can be generated to offset that outlay and produce a profit then, as factory after factory found, it was better to leave bus making to others. In that of course buses were no different to any other kind of commodity; where they did differ was in the nature of the potential buyers, for as the years progressed buying power became concentrated into fewer and fewer hands, while individual fleet sizes grew even larger. So, for a manufacturer upon whom the sun shone, a single model might sell by the thousand at satisfactory profit, and with little effort after the original sales presentations. Less fortunate competitors, meanwhile, would be working hard to sell every unit of an equally meritorious chassis.

Just as in the case of freight carrying vehicles it was the legislative changes of the early 1930s which formed the great divide between ancient and modern history in bus design. Indeed the trend had already been set, since pneumatic tyres had reached a stage where they could be used for bus work four or five years before they could be generally used on lorries. And, as with lorries, cool-running pneumatic tyres meant that vehicle speeds could be considerably increased and that vehicle components could be made much lighter. Again in common with lorries the changes were made to components rather than overall concepts: chassis still had engines at the front, and vertically mounted, while drive was transmitted to the rear axle (during a short-lived fashion for six-wheeled buses) through a clutch and gearbox. One noticeable but relatively insignificant change was that during the late 1920s nearly all drivers of full-sized buses moved to a position beside their engines, thereby giving rise to the characteristic half-cab layout.

Through the all-pervading influence of one designer, who worked first for one and then the other, the Leyland-AEC axis was already dominating the market with its ranges of Titans, Regents, and their derivatives before the law changed. Despite often bitter rivalry it was a domination they were never to yield and their successes in competition with each other and everyone else pointed up yet again the wisdom of having the right product at the right time. Guy in particular had reason to resent their success for it had produced modern high speed chassis well before either Leyland or AEC. But Guy had been just a little too early for the market, while Maudslay, in addition to making the same error, was simply too small and feeble to capitalise on its enterprise.

In the wake of the two giants the rest became hardly more than also-rans. Before, say, 1928 a lorry maker could soften chassis suspensions, alter back axle gear ratios, and sell the results for bus work. After that time, and increasingly, the two markets became ever more widely separated: Albion, Thornycroft, Halley, Crossley, Bristol, Guy, Morris, Sunbeam, Daimler, Maudslay, and others all produced bus chassis intended to rival Leyland and AEC but they were all overshadowed. Some, notably Albion and Guy, built up loyal if localised followings and made bus work worthwhile. Bristol was fortunate in that it could rely on a steady demand from fellow members of the railways-controlled Tilling group, which also dominated about half of the nominally

private bus companies in Britain. Daimler had the good sense to early realise that bus making in the modern style could be compatible with making luxury private cars, its other staple, and earned for itself a commanding position in the supply of buses to municipally-owned fleets.

Crossley tried to do likewise but Daimler and Leyland, not to mention AEC, left little room among the corporations and councils for a fourth supplier to prosper. As for the others: Morris, that giant of the motor industry, found that there simply was not enough room for another brand of motor bus; Thornycroft gave the impression of not being wholehearted about buses and fared accordingly; Halley was in its death throes; Sunbeam (so far as motor buses were concerned) likewise; and Maudslay retreated into supplying the sort of operator who bought vehicles in ones, twos, and threes.

At the lighter end of the market, which had once found room for Austins, Morrises, Stars, Albions, Guys, Beans, and many another chassis of similar kind, operator loyalties transferred wholesale to cheap mass-produced vehicles, most of American origin, which offered excellent value for money. While several of the others maintained a presence in the market none of them came near to rivalling the Americans. Price must have been a major cause and perhaps the error made by Leyland, Guy, Morris, and one or two others was that of incorporating too much hand-built quality into products intended for customers who had no need for it.

Although, no doubt, they appreciated the rapid advances in comfort and speed that resulted from the efforts of chassis makers, very few bus passengers knew or know who made the mechanical parts of the vehicles. In the nature of things bus chassis are well concealed from public view, and with the passing of distinctive radiator shapes they became quite anonymous. Even fewer passengers, no doubt, give so much as a passing thought to the concerns which made the bodywork they ride in, although here too advances in techniques were rapid and profound.

While vehicles remained both small and slow,

The chassis is an AEC, but it might as well have been any of a dozen other makes, for the chars-a-banc which opened up post-1919 coaching were usually based on lorry chassis. Not infrequently lorries were used to carry goods in one body on weekdays, and passengers in another at weekends. Although the term remained in common use for decades this is not really a char-a-banc: that label should be applied only to vehicles which had rows of seats across the vehicle, and a separate entrance to each row. This specimen, with its deep bucket seats, has begun the long journey to modernity with its centre aisle and a hood that could be rolled forward on rails mounted on the body sides.

Left: A Daimler of 1934 demonstrating the always spectacular business of tilt-testing a double-decked bus. British law requires that such vehicles, appropriately loaded upstairs with sand-bags, will remain stable at an angle of 28 deg: close inspection of this one shows that although the front tyre seems firmly planted, the rear outer has daylight beneath it. Single deckers must achieve 35 deg, and it is this stipulation which gave rise to many of the so-called double-decked coaches of the early 1980s: there is small prospect of these high floorline single deckers reaching 35 deg, but the addition of a handful of seats in what was meant to be luggage space gives them the 28 deg loophole.

Below left: Before – and after – their bold attempt to break into the market for full-sized buses, the Morris-Commercial organisation could not be regarded as a force in the passenger service vehicle business. Of course an operator would occasionally use a more or less modified lorry chassis, and indeed the company actually offered a passenger chassis which bore marked indications of its goods origins. It was the post-1948 version of this which Morris Motors used for transporting its famous works brass band. By adopting the $1\frac{1}{2}$ deck layout for the body ample space was provided under the rear raised floor for the band instruments.

Below right: Mechanically the chassis were crude, the external appearance ungainly, and performance on the road barely adequate even for the requirements of the day. But coaches built before 1914 were sometimes fitted out and trimmed in a style more usually found only in the most luxurious of luxury cars. Not all of them of course: the saloons of nearly all double and single-decked buses were as austere as those of the horse buses they were dispossessing, but as this Daimler of 1913 shows, once given their heads, coach-builders could do a great deal to draw the attention of passengers away from solid tyres, rough roads, and juddering clutches.

By the end of the 1950s few of the once conventional heavy single-decked chassis with front vertical engines were being made in Britain, and those were intended for export: the under-floor-engined, high-framed kind had taken over completely. Yet this operator had need of vehicles capable of passing under very low bridges, and in the absence of a suitable chassis turned instead to AEC Regent double deckers, on which specially low single-decked bodies were built by Roe. This was the last model in a long line of Regents and (in its intended form) sold well until the rear-engined invasion overwhelmed it. This last AEC radiator grille shape is said to have been inspired by contemporary Rover car designs.

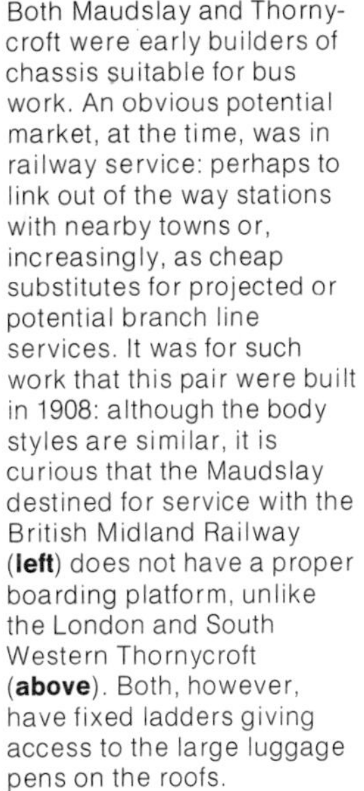

Both Maudslay and Thornycroft were early builders of chassis suitable for bus work. An obvious potential market, at the time, was in railway service: perhaps to link out of the way stations with nearby towns or, increasingly, as cheap substitutes for projected or potential branch line services. It was for such work that this pair were built in 1908: although the body styles are similar, it is curious that the Maudslay destined for service with the British Midland Railway (**left**) does not have a proper boarding platform, unlike the London and South Western Thornycroft (**above**). Both, however, have fixed ladders giving access to the large luggage pens on the roofs.

By 1956 Leyland had consolidated its thinking on rear-engined double deckers and in collaboration with MCW produced a complete vehicle for evaluation and demonstration. It was of semi-integral construction: while the floor and running units were self-supporting, the body structure was expected to take much of the loading. The vehicle, not yet complete – the front roof dome has still to be trimmed and glazed, and other details are missing – shows the seemingly odd window pillar arrangement which was adopted: it concealed essential bracing. But the industry was not yet ready for integral buses of any kind, and production Atlanteans had separate chassis frames.

traditional hand-crafted bodybuilding methods were good enough, but the rapid advances from the mid-1920s onwards rapidly outstripped available skills and materials and required in their stead something more nearly approaching that of engineering. By careful calculation and design it proved possible to make bodywork strong and durable, and all at a reasonable weight. From all-timber, with metal bracing, bus bodybuilders had moved by the 1920s into composite structures which combined wooden framing with steel or light alloy panelling. Carefully arranging the jointing caused the panels to brace and stiffen the frames, and this form of construction proved suitable for all kinds of vehicles. Indeed, it became almost universal, and because of the relatively low cost of tooling and other facilities required to manufacture it Leyland, Guy, and others found it worthwhile to set up their own bodyshops and offer customers a choice of chassis to be bodied elsewhere, or vehicles completed under one roof.

While Leyland and Guy both had thriving body-building shops AEC never made bodies. For years its main customer was London, which made many of its own, and in later times AEC bought Park Royal and Roe, both of them long established in the business. Indeed, a considerable factor in the decision to take control of Crossley was the well accepted system owned by that company for making all-metal (or more accurately metal-framed) bodies.

Metal frames took the trend to properly stressed and engineered structures much further, adding a considerable bonus in the ease with which replacement parts could be inserted. Inevitably the large firms took it up, and equally inevitably the smaller ones faded away. Even Leyland, which had marketed metal frames for some years, withdrew in favour of the specialists, although later adventures with integral and chassisless construction, which have the effect of removing the need for a separate self-supporting chassis frame, brought the company back first into close co-operation with bodybuilders, and then with the National, into bodymaking proper.

A study in double deckers. Crossley, Daimler, Bristol, Albion and AEC products of the 1930s show clearly how the attempts by body-builders to introduce some uniformity – witness the upper decks – were undermined by the absence of common dimensioning for engine length and radiator positioning. Minor differences in wheelbases and chassis frame heights made it very difficult to exchange bodies between chassis. This undesirable variety was dealt a major blow during the war years, and later.

The original Leyland Titan of 1927 was not quite the first double decker in the modern idiom: Guy could perhaps lay claim to that. But it instantly became the standard against which all others were measured. Leyland Motors pursued the Titan theme with vigour. From it stemmed a family of medium and full-sized buses, and another of lorries. Nor was the Titan itself allowed to stagnate, for new versions followed at frequent intervals over 30 years – not that there was much wrong with individual models, but Leyland had no intention of letting others catch up. Pictured is the 1932 torque converter demonstrator in Sheffield.

Never before (or since) was a new model tested quite so thoroughly as the London Transport, AEC, Park Royal, Routemaster. Once the overall design was finalised two slave vehicles were assembled and put to work. Loosely resembling lorries (**below**), they were loaded to represent double deckers in service and for many months worked on London bus routes, faithfully shadowing fare-carrying vehicles, including stopping at all the stops. In the event few significant changes were needed once production vehicles entered service although front end styling was much improved from that displayed by Routemaster 1 (**below right**), on the AEC stand at the 1954 Commercial Motor Show.

The AEC-controlled group of companies scored a notable success when it produced the integral Routemaster for London. This double decker proved to be an outstanding machine and led incidentally to Park Royal becoming a vehicle maker, as distinct from a mere bodier of other peoples' chassis. Routemasters were supplied

Left and below left:
Materials shortages dictated that the 'utility' double deckers produced during the Second World War by Bristol, Guy and Daimler were reduced to essentials, and unladen weight rose as heavier materials had to be used. The result was surprising: not only did the vehicles give troublefree service during the war, but they went on for years afterwards – to all appearances being indestructable. It was an object lesson in what mechanical simplicity could achieve. Granted, on many the bodywork soon fell off, mortally stricken by rot attacking poor and unseasoned timber, but many of the chassis were later fitted with new postwar bodies and continued to give satisfaction.

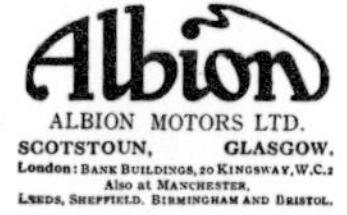

30/60 h.p. Bus, one of a number of Albions owned by the Halifax Corporation.

ALBIONS MAKE A GOING CONCERN A <u>PAYING</u> CONCERN

ALBIONS will make *your* Bus service a paying concern as they have already done for many of the biggest and most successful passenger-carrying enterprises in the country. Their exceptionally low running and maintenance costs will start saving you money right away.

And Albions will go on saving you money because their reliability will reduce your bills for repairs and replacements, and lessen the risk of delays and breakdowns on the road.

Let us send you a chassis for inspection. 30/60 h.p. 4-cylinder Buses and 36/90 h.p. "Viking Six" Buses seating 29 or 32 passengers. Also the "Victor" 20-passenger and the "Valkyrie" 4-cylinder 32-passenger Buses.

Write to-day for full particulars.

See the Albion Exhibit **STAND 38** at the Commercial Vehicle Show Olympia 5-14 November

Albion
ALBION MOTORS LTD.
SCOTSTOUN, GLASGOW.
London: BANK BUILDINGS, 20 KINGSWAY, W.C.2
Also at MANCHESTER.
LEEDS, SHEFFIELD, BIRMINGHAM AND BRISTOL.

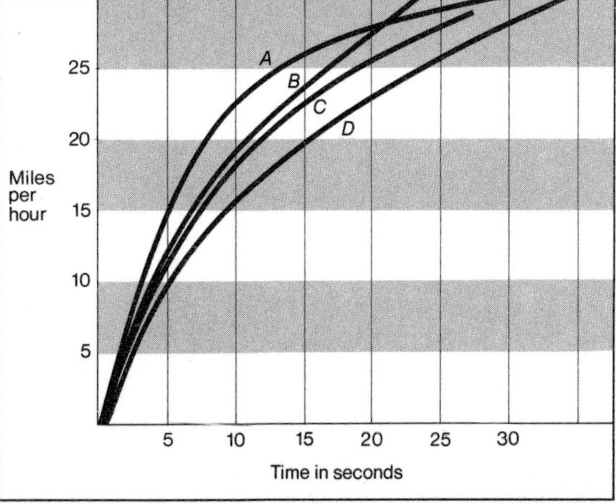

In 1937 Leyland conducted a series of performance tests with a six-wheeled London trolley bus and comparable petrol-engined vehicles. In acceleration the trolley bus, **A** in the graph, comfortably outperformed a Titan, **B**, fitted with a torque converter; a Titanic, **C**, with a torque converter; and **D**, a Titanic with conventional gearbox. The relatively poor performance of the six-wheeled motor buses compared with the Titan, which had a similar engine, reflects their greater weight and therefore lower drive axle ratios. But it is clear why the Lysholm-Smith automatic transmission won some acceptance in 'Gearless' vehicles, until of course the rate at which it consumed fuel became a significant factor.

with AEC or Leyland running gear – although at that time the two were still rivals – and the combination of talents became yet more firmly cemented in more recent years when some of the thinking that coalesced as the Leyland Titan proved to have been derived from Routemaster, intermarried with Leyland's own Atlantean – and with more than a hint of Bristol VR and Daimler Fleetline. The thing went further, in that before entering full-scale production in the National factory, early Titan specimens were made at the Park Royal works, and even a few at Roe.

Another notable marriage of interests was Bristol and Eastern Coach Works, for both concerns belonged first to Tilling and then to the State. A natural tendency during the first condition to work closely together was reinforced by law during the second, when neither partner was allowed to sell to any operator that was not also State-owned. The result of this enforced colla-boration led to some outstanding designs in all kinds of bus and coach, including some chassis-less vehicles.

When in 1939 war came again its effects on bus makers was both predictable and disconcerting. Only to be expected was the immediate ban on bus manufacture in favour of producing war material, and also to be expected was the sub-sequent partial lifting of that ban in order that war workers might have the means of travelling to their work. Several manufacturers were able to assemble a few chassis from pre-war parts stocks but the designated builders of heavy utility vehicles turned out to be Guy, and later Daimler and Bristol.

There was some logic in choosing Bristol, which had not made lorries for years, and which was a specialised and almost captive supplier. Because of its marketing policy Daimler was almost a captive too, but Guy had bowed out of the heavy bus business some years before. The result was that many of the hard-pressed operators deemed to be deserving of new chassis found themselves having to accept vehicles which were largely unfamiliar to them. Indeed even those companies which had previously bought Daimler or Bristol, or who remembered Guy, found little they recognised in these wartime products. Specifications were cut to the bone: light alloys were almost entirely absent; and the use of all kinds of materials was reduced to a minimum. Yet these spartan machines soon won an undying loyalty from fleet engineers for their simplicity and reliability and many lasted for twenty years or more. In that respect if in no other they resembled the subvention chassis of the previous war. However, the bodywork fitted to austerity bus chassis not only looked but was harsh and uncomfortable. The best that can be said of it is

that the bodybuilders used little material, and that of such poor quality that generally it hardly outlasted the war years, thus giving way to the much more attractive and durable structures which a great many of the chassis later carried.

The trading pattern of the 1930s continued, broadly, through the first post-war decade until the mid-1950s. Despite considerable success in opening up export markets overall vehicle design had hardly moved forward during the intervening years, and the divergence between British and foreign bus design was widening rapidly. One cause was the continuing home market pre-occupation with double deckers, a type which had limited appeal elsewhere in the world, and also with two-man crews. In single deckers it is true there had been forward movement, for in a headlong rush every maker who saw a future in bus manufacture had put on the market underfloor-engined designs. In the 1950s buyers could choose from Leyland, or Guy, or AEC, or Daimler, or AEC's dubiously badge-engineered as Maudslay or Crossley, or several other makes. The overall advantages of uncluttered floor lines and higher seating capacities quite obscured the fact that American and German operators had been able to buy such vehicles fifteen years earlier, and were now moving on to rear-mounted engines and integral construction.

When the real change in domestic buying habits arrived it did so swiftly and devastatingly, caused by simultaneous explosions of car and television ownership. In 1950 the bus industry had seemed secure; in 1960 it appeared to be for all intents and purposes on the brink of extinction. In a desperate attempt to stem the haemorrhage, one-man operation soon became the norm, and the need to provide easy access for passengers to the driver caused Leyland to redouble its attempts to rethink the layout of double-decked vehicles.

The Leyland National, a carefully thought out structure, is assembled with jigs and tools that reduce labour content to a minimum and ensure a high degree of accuracy. Sides, roofs, and ends are built up separately before being put together (**left**), and the engine and running units are almost the last items to be fitted into otherwise almost completed vehicles. Within the confines of the basic structure many variations can be made, apart from vehicle lengths, power units, seating and trim. One drastic modification was a ramped front entrance for airport work (**below**); in another, National sub-assemblies are being incorporated in lightweight rail cars (see page 113).

Most of the original bonneted Comets were for goods transport, but Leyland recognised a continuing need in overseas markets for a bus in which the engine was readily accessible. The Comet was well suited to such changes as were necessary, and it could take up to 35 seats. On the home market there was then, in the 1940s and 1950s, a requirement for a smaller bus in which the driver could easily collect fares: most such were built on cheap mass-produced chassis, but a few Comets entered this kind of service. Even fewer were built as touring coaches, for this was a market strictly segregated into large capacity, good quality vehicles and low capacity, low priced ones.

An incidental advantage of the once-universal practice of building double deckers as, virtually, two single-decked bodies was the relative ease of shipping export vehicles. Not that many went abroad that way, but as with this 1938 Weymann-bodied AEC trolley bus for Cape Town, it was sometimes possible to economise on shipping space and therefore cost. Apart from the large number of opening windows the vehicle bears a close resemblance to contemporaries operating in Britain – and particularly therefore to those of London Transport, which set the pattern for third generation trolleys, those of the 1930s onwards.

With a separate fare-collecting conductor there was no useful way of converting the area beside the driver into passenger accommodation. There was, therefore, no need to introduce mechanical complications by placing the engine anywhere other than its traditional location. The new order of things changed all that, and Leyland took the bold step of removing the power unit to the extreme rear and mounting it across the frame, driving forward to the back axle in just the same way that General Motors had been doing with single deckers in America since the early 1930s.

Daimler quickly followed with what was virtually a carbon copy of the Leyland design and after some delay Bristol too took to the rear transverse-mounted engine layout for its 'deckers. AEC by 1960 had lost the spirit of enterprise which had once characterised its career, and in any case its impending absorption into Leyland was to stop all original work. By this time the bus business was in such a parlous state that no one else even tried.

There had been earlier attempts to break out of the conventional double-decked mould: AEC stunned the British-orientated bus world in the early 1930s with a handsome and strikingly modern design which placed the engine longitudinally behind the driver; in the 1950s Guy tried with indifferent success to combine front engines and front entrances; and Bristol built some vehicles which had their power units longitudinally mounted but behind the right side rear wheel. Since a handful of operators, seeking standardisation, also bought rear-engined chassis and put single-decked bodies on them, trends in single decker design became harder to discern – par-

ticularly after Leyland, AEC, Bristol, and others adopted underfloor-mounted engines at the extreme rear. This arrangement, it turned out, was to have durability and since it was adopted for the Leyland National may be said to have become a definitive form.

All the while the variety of models and makes available to buyers became less and less. Both Austin and Morris had offered passenger versions of otherwise conventional light lorry chassis, but after their merging quietly abandoned what small position they once held. After its control passed to Leyland, Albion tried to build up a minor business with cleverly designed lightweights of a kind not made elsewhere in the group, but success was not such as to encourage new models. Daimler, after it joined Jaguar, soon became a one-model firm, offering only its rear-engined chassis. Guy, virtually at a standstill when Jaguar moved in, concentrated thereafter on one range of heavy lorries. Bristol maintained a comprehensive catalogue until recent years, but when the time came for heavy investment in new models it found, just as AEC had done twenty years earlier, and Maudslay, and Crossley, and Star, and many others before that, that membership of a group inevitably leads to the making of common cause and the suppression of individuality. The glories of earlier years could be no more, and when variety was again offered to British operators it came, in disconcerting quantities, from highly competitive importers.

Probably the largest buses ever built to the once-conventional front engine and half cab layout were the six-wheeled Guys bought by the Johannesburg transport authority in 1960. The overall length of 34 ft 6 in is now regularly exceeded by other kinds of bus, but the 20 ft wheelbase of these giants added to the impression of sheer size. Seats for 85 passengers were provided within an overall capacity of 106: Bus Bodies of South Africa produced the bodywork. Although well able to do the work for which they were intended, it is evident that later forms of high capacity vehicle, notably rear-engined double deckers and articulated vehicles, would be more convenient in traffic.

Above left: Working much in the Routemaster mould AEC and Park Royal produced their Bridgemaster, a chassisless minimum height double decker. By 1960 the demand for forward entrance double deckers was increasing as a result of the theory that mobile conductors could not be expected to supervise passenger safety on a 30 ft long bus with rear entrance. But it made a clumsy arrangement: the flight of steps necessary to gain entrance are hidden in this view, but it shows the obtrusive bulge of the transmission housing between entrance and stair foot. The rear-engined Atlantean and Fleetline provided a better solution – and were virtually the only answer when one-man operation became general.

Above right: Albion built a worthwhile number of double deckers but so far as total sales were concerned it was never in the AEC, Leyland, or Daimler league. A main reason was that the company strongholds were in parts of the country that did not have much use for the double decker – and in many cases have little use for it still. Most sales therefore had to be worked for, so perhaps the 'Venturer' model name was appropriate after all. There was a single-decked equivalent too, the Valiant. This Venturer entered service in 1950, but there was no room within Leyland for a competitor to the Titan, and Albion enterprise in this direction was stifled.

While the mechanically similar Titan was making major inroads into urban bus fleets its single-decked version, the first Tiger, was doing much the same with coach operators. Coach rather than bus, because the Tiger possessed more power than the generality of stage carriage work required. But it was ideal for exploiting the long distance express services which were springing up in Britain, and elsewhere in the world too, in the early 1930s. Despite considerable internal luxury this Tiger demonstrates a characteristic of its time: bodywork that was almost standard bus.

The last great success for AEC in the passenger vehicle world was the Reliance, which first entered production in 1953 and remained a best seller for a quarter of a century. Other models came and went, but the Reliance went on, finally becoming the last all-AEC to be made by British Leyland. Over the years one version or another was under every kind of single-decked vehicle, but most went for long-distance coaching. This Reliance is carrying an example of the once-popular Burlingham Seagull body, perhaps one of the finest looking structures ever to be built, and one particularly well suited to mid-underfloor engined chassis of this kind.

Vans

Centre: Trojans, as originally conceived, were full of sound ideas: their misfortune was that the overall package had been designed without sufficient thought being given to their acceptability. There was, for example, a one-piece underframe, almost punt-like in appearance, which took the place of ordinary chassis frames. And because the suspension was remarkably supple, expensive and troublesome pneumatic tyres need not be used. Two-stroke engines contain far less working parts than equivalent four-strokes, so the Trojan had a two-stroke power unit – which lay flat in the underframe. It appealed to some van operators, including the British post office in 1924.

Below: Many of the apparent advantages of articulation in small vehicles can be realised only in operations where several units are required and uncoupling is both quick and easy. Then semi-trailers can be left for loading and unloading while the tractor is busy elsewhere: it was the classic pattern of one tractor and three semi-trailers established long before by Scammell, with its Mechanical Horse. This 1964 demonstrator, using a BMC J4 with Morris label, shows a type of small articulated that has made fitful appearances over the years. Most potential operators, on due reflection, decide that similar cubic capacity can be achieved on rigid chassis – with less operating inconvenience.

Austin Seven vans of the early 1920s often showed clearly the horsey leanings of their constructors and users. There was something about the Austin baby which could easily bring on severe attacks of whimsy, and in an age when mobile advertisements were common this vehicle (**left**) seemed to suffer more than most. The 1932 detached residence (**below right**) is typical. By 1939 the old Seven had finally run its course, to be replaced by the new 8 hp car (**right**) with more bodyspace, and in the modern panel van idiom. It was just in time to be made in large numbers for war service.

A contrast in production lines. When, in 1908, the Wolseley shop (**bottom**) stopped work for the camera, the company was nearing its peacetime height. Apart from passenger cars it had a successful range of taxi cab models and a chassis suitable for lorries or double-decked buses. These cab chassis have two-cylinder engines: the curious drop-frames permitted a reasonably low entrance step for passengers. This is the factory which later produced heavy Morris-Commercials. By 1940 light van production at Morris was taking great advantage of sheet steel pressing techniques, and moving assembly lines. This model (**below**) was derived from the Series E 8 hp car, and together they survived until the post-war Minor.

Rival products from the main two components of BMC illustrate well the difficulties they had in turning small cars into sufficiently roomy vans. The Austin (**left**) has a neat unified look, the Morris body (**right**) is clearly an added box. User preference was illustrated by the much longer production life of the latter – until 1971. Both models were finalised before BMC came into being but it was found that the Austin engine was the better of the two and was used in both. Sales of such light vans was artificially encouraged by British tax legislation that made them much cheaper to buy than their equivalent car models.

Standard was never a major force in the world of light commercials. When car business was slack a model or two might be tried, but were never allowed to distract attention from the company's main trade. But inevitably Standard chassis were sometimes fitted with goods bodywork: the neat little traveller's coupé (**above right**) of 1913 is typical of a class of vehicle now quite gone, replaced by large-booted family cars that do not betray their drivers' calling. Immediately before the Standard Vanguard era, which began in 1948, and included a factory-built van and pick-up, the company reintroduced some pre-1939 models. Among them was the Flying 12, and a handful of vans, including this one (**above**), were built for Ferguson tractor dealers. The Asprey van (**above left**), of 1954, was essentially a Standard 10.

Morris Motors – an entity distinct from Morris-Commercial – could expect to sell enough light trucks to make mass-production assembly well worthwhile, even though the designs were often only indirectly linked to the passenger car range. The smallest of this pair of Morris models is the 5 cwt 8 hp (**below**), which owed much to early Minors and sold well throughout the 1930s. So highly did the British postal authorities think of it that the styling stayed in production just for them, for years. Bonnets used to be allowed to occupy a great deal of small vehicle lengths: in a commendable effort to minimise overall dimensions without reducing load space the driving position of this 1936 8-10 cwt model (**below left**) was moved forward in a manner subsequently followed by rival best-sellers.

In their quite distinct ways the 15-20 cwt Morris-Commercial PV (**centre right**) and its Austin contemporary, the 25 cwt three-way van (**above**), both epitomised their era, the post-war late 1940s. The PV (which had first put in an appearance just before the war) was simple in design and austere almost to an extreme. Usually made in panel van form, the poor materials then available led to rapid body decay. But if the Morris-Commercial symbolised austerity and hard times, the sides and rear-loading Austin had a more florid look that seemed to anticipate a better future. But not for itself: within BMC the future for this kind of vehicle lay with derivatives of Morris products.

BCG 276 J

Most Morris Minors intended for commercial use had factory van bodies, but an appreciable number were built as general purpose pick-up trucks.

Right: The A40 was to Austin what the Minor was to the pre-British Motor Corporation Morris. Like the Minor all three basic forms – saloon car, van, and pick-up – had a 'family' look, but although eagerly bought in the car-hungry late 1940s, the Minor proved to have longer lasting appeal. One reason was the distinct approaches to design: while the Austin was very much one step forward in conventional small car thinking, and therefore appeared cramped, the Morris leapt into a new era. It too was small – but it was also roomy. There is a certain irony in the latter-day popularity of imported pick-ups, when native factories have offered them for years, and sold few.

The British Motor Corporation Mini, introduced to meet a perceived threat from the 1950s craze for 'bubble' cars, was soon followed by van and pick-up versions. Although ostensibly meant for commercial use, British car taxation laws led to a great many being bought for private use, but despite the carrying capacity being limited by restricted volume rather than weight carrying ability the Mini secured a niche as runabouts from which it has yet to be dislodged. Like other BMC-origin products the Mini has undergone bewildering changes of identity, ranging from being the smallest unit bearing the Leyland name to being a marque in its own right.

Below left: The Royal Flying Corps Crossley tender is an example of that rare and select breed: the vehicular immortals. Thousands were made and they served the British flying services of the First World War as general purpose runabouts. Although essentially cars in concept they were large and quite powerful and when their military service was completed many re-entered service in the civilian world. Here they proved just as reliable and often long lived: conversion to vans was commonplace – and some became small buses. Their twinned wire wheels were a distinct novelty.

So many of the Morris-derived LD vans produced by the British Motor Corporation went to the British postal authorities, that some thought it was a model made exclusively for them. But the LD was on general sale, and for most of the 1950s and 1960s. Two capacities were made, for one ton and 30 cwt loads, and the vast majority were good-looking vans which generally resembled this postal unit. One of the last product changes initiated by BMC was the replacement of the highly regarded LD by the EA – which did not attract similar esteem.

Among the confusion of light vans already produced by BMC and sold as Austins or Morrises, the Austin division, in the late 1960s, thought it could see a niche that might be filled by a van version of the 1100 car. In fact it was hardly more than an Austin Countryman/Morris Traveller estate without the side windows, but the characteristics of the Hydrolastic suspension were unsuited to van work. Overcoming these difficulties was deemed to be impracticable and after some prototype work the project was dropped. Another major drawback would have been the low roofline: the box-like Morris Minor looked unfashionable throughout its long life, but it provided a convenient and roomy means of transport.

Buses were usually almost a sideline to Albion, but an appreciable number of conventional heavy chassis were made. Later, for Leyland, lightweights were built.

No Fuss by Bus

Considering the apparent advantages of speed in ambulances, it took a long time for motor vehicles to entirely supplant horse transport. Perhaps there were lingering doubts about the starting reliability of such emergency vehicles. From the constructional point of view a great difficulty was and remains the small numbers of units required: usually, therefore, manufacturing economics have dictated the use of modified light commercial chassis. The Wolseley (**below**), built in 1913 for naval dockyard use, was essentially a truck chassis, suitably bodied, and so was the 1960 BMC (**right**). This, however, was fitted with air suspension in place of the usual leaf springs.

While other makers were producing elegantly shaped bodywork for their medium vans BMC, toward the end of its separate existence, assumed that users would on the whole prefer more generally useful boxes, in which hardly any space could not be put to good use. In addition, to keep overall length to a minimum, the short bonnets used by others would be avoided, and since across-cab access would be a useful selling point the engine – petrol or diesel – would therefore be inclined under the cab floor. The result was indeed a motorised box, with flat vertical sides; the only incursion into load space was the low wheel boxes (**left**). And by inclining the power unit not only was the cab floor flat, but there was easy access into the body, too (**below**).

Harrods for more than money can buy
LONDON TRANSPORT
RM1933

The Park Royal Routemaster was the final word in rear platform double-decked bus design. Its integral body was built almost entirely in light alloys. The two pictured are in special liveries to mark LT's Golden Jubilee in 1983.

One-offs and specials

Very few companies in the commercial vehicle manufacturing world have contrived to expand and thrive while building only unusual vehicles, special designs, and one-offs. To be sure it has been done, but the overwhelming majority of makers decided in their earliest years that common prudence dictated they should persevere in the mass market places; regularly obtaining five or ten per cent of a market comprising thousands of vehicles will almost certainly be a sounder foundation for a long trading life than holding fifty or sixty per cent of a market that is annually only a few dozen units strong.

In large part-assembly lines, economies are those of scale, for the longer the production run of a standard design the quicker and easier each 'build' becomes. When a factory concentrates on making specialised designs with a high proportion of unique features to be incorporated in each vehicle, costs rise very quickly indeed even when the main components are readily obtainable at reasonable prices.

None of the companies now part of the Leyland Vehicles group ever concentrated wholly on building special purpose chassis but inevitably over the years nearly all of them at one time or another were tempted into making excursions in that direction. Sometimes local loyalties played a part, as when Scammell made some fire appliances for its home town of Watford. Occasionally a specific development contract would lead a company into unfamiliar paths: various military authorities persuaded Thornycroft, Guy, Crossley, and others to make some machines that were

very strange indeed. Not infrequently a manufacturer identified surplus capacity in its own factories and sought to fill the gap with a product somewhat out of character – which was how AEC found itself making large off-road dump trucks. Just occasionally original thought on the subject of a well-established need led makers into – usually – disastrous attempts to change the course of development. The early, and peculiar, twin-engined integrally-built double-decked Daimler bus, mounted on bicycle-like suspension wheels, is a case in point.

Scammell was not alone in feeling that perhaps money might be made with fire appliances, vehicles which traditionally are tailored to meet specific local requirements and which incorporate much expensive ancillary equipment. Albion often collaborated with specialist makers and Leyland kept a thriving sideline going until in the vehicle famine days of the 1940s and 1950s it let the business drop in favour of making ever greater numbers of ordinary lorries and buses. Leyland bus chassis, like those of other makers, often found favour with specialist fire appliance builders and when Leyland made what may well be its last determined attempt to corner for itself a share of the market, with its Firemaster of 1958, the main running components were again from a contemporary passenger chassis, the underfloor-engined Worldmaster. When AEC, in the days of its independence, sold a considerable number of appliance chassis they too used bus running units, which were assembled at the Maudslay plant.

Probably the greatest single contribution by AEC to original thought in the matter of bus design was the Q-type of the mid-1930s. Generally it was a company that exploited convention: in putting the Q-type engine vertically behind the driver it did something no one had done before. The overall objects included better weight distribution over the wheels, and a more un-cluttered chassis for body-builders to work on. As this double-decked sample shows, most of the latter advantage was wasted in the days before one-man operation, while the neces-sary length of driveline coupled with legal restric-tions on overall length simply transferred overhang from the rear to the front.

Only the more spectacular kinds of fire fighting appliance really need purpose-built carrying chassis, for many vehicles are hardly more than special bodies on otherwise quite ordinary pro-duction vehicles, and both Austin and Morris, and then the Leyland products derived from them, obtained their fair share of such work. But one breed of fire fighter which is very special indeed are the airfield crash tenders, a market that Thornycroft made much its own. The combination of high gross weight, tremendous performance on road or across country, and high quality bespoke engineering made them natural subjects for a firm like Thornycroft and in the fullness of time Scam-mell, where descendants of the one-time Thorny-crofts are now made. At the other end of the scale, yet also required to perform in much the same conditions and with the same unfailing reliability, are the many fire tenders built on Land Rover and Range Rover chassis. An appreciable number of both have each had an extra axle added at the back in order to increase carrying capacity.

Not many steam-propelled fire appliances were made, and those only at the very beginning of motor transport. Experience over the previous forty years or so had shown that while the pumps could certainly project a stream of water in a highly satisfactory manner, the time and attend-ance needed to keep steam power always avail-able could be tolerated for only so long as nothing better was available. Petrol engines soon became very much better. At the other end of the glamour

What should have been a precursor of several desirable developments was the Leyland lowloading trolley bus of 1935. By adopt-ing the often tried but yet to be accepted device of using twin motors and a split drive, with the propeller shafts outside the chassis side-members, a very low floor level was achieved in the lower saloon. Only one step was required, and the overall height was nearly a foot lower than conventional height double deckers – with full headroom upstairs. But buyers preferred convention; no more were made.

Leyland also made six-wheeled bus chassis, even though demand was such as to hardly justify calling them production models. The City Coach Company used a fleet of 18 built in the mid-1930s on an express route and thought so highly of them that several were rebodied into the form shown (**above**) in 1947. Leyland was also the first serious experi-menter with twin-steering six-wheelers, an arrange-ment which overcame most of the objections to three axles – apart from the extra weight. A double-decked trolley bus was built, and used for many years in London; for single-decked work there was this front-engined Gnu (**left**) with set back front axles and also a solitary underfloor-engined Panda, all three of the late 1930s.

GRAND
PROVIDENT
EXHIBITION CUM SALE
WB8 1492

Buses articulated in lorry style are rare. Even rarer are double-decked artics, which have been produced by the Leyland India factory for local use.

Sometimes an operator discovers a need which somehow has not been foreseen by vehicle makers. Sometimes the needs change, and vehicle owners are not willing to buy entirely new transport; not infrequently a wish to create something original or distinctive reaches fulfilment. The result is a special. In catalogue form the Leyland Bison was a rigid six-wheeler, but the addition of an extra steering axle turned this New Zealand tipper (**left**) into a lightweight eight-wheeler. The recovery vehicle (**right**) was once a rear-steering AEC Mammoth Minor tractor, but with a Matador front axle added, it has become a rather special four by four.

scale, where the equally essential cesspool and gully emptiers laboured, steam had the great advantage that with its aid a powerful suction could be produced – and without the need for mechanical pumps containing wearing parts. Leyland built some steam-powered cesspit emptiers in the years before the First World War, and many of such sales as Fowler made of its not very successful steam waggon during the 1920s were fitted out for this humble but necessary task. Indeed this commercial enterprise led to the basic equipment continuing to be offered for fitting to other chassis, including some Albions of the 1930s, after Fowler had quit the steamer business.

Quite often an operator would also have sprinkler bars fitted to cesspool emptiers so that the quite high capacity tankers could also be used for street washing; indeed, in earlier times purpose-built sprinklers were common, but the arrival of properly sealed road surfaces and the departure of horse transport have largely made the sprinkler (often with an attendant small crowd of street urchins frolicking under the spray) into no more than a memory of city summers past.

Elsewhere among the vehicles used to provide public health services, street sweeping has almost always been the province of manufacturers who do little else, so specialised is the application. In latter years, so expensive has it become to make original chassis designs, most machines have come to be based on standard production chassis which are modified to a greater or lesser degree to fit them for the role. Leyland group chassis have not often been so used (although Thornycrofts in the 1930s and 1940s were sometimes used as the basis for sweepers) and hardly more frequently for urban door to door refuse collecting. In fact, of the Leyland group companies only Guy, among the internal combustion-engined vehicle makers, made a determined attempt in this field of activity and achieved a fair measure of success in the 1920s with a range of specially adapted chassis fitted with small diameter wheels. A desirable feature, this, when all bins were lifted by hand and contained a high proportion of heavy ash from solid fuel domestic heating. Quite often chassis from the cheaper mass-produced ranges have found favour in rural collecting, where sophistication is deemed unnecessary and first cost is a consideration, but these are usually hardly more than standard chassis with closed bodywork added.

For many years battery-electric power had things very much its own way in urban municipal transport: from about 1920 until the mid-1950s. Some large vehicles were made, the requirements of the work matching well the performance characteristics of battery power, and Electricar built some sizeable fleets of up to four tons capacity vehicles during the years between the wars. The company also collaborated with Scammell in producing some electric Mechanical Horse municipal vehicles. In more recent times the nature of domestic refuse has changed considerably, and while the need was once for vehicles easily loaded by hand and suitable for carrying dense low volume cargo now the demand is for chassis able to carry heavy and complicated bodywork that can compact low density, high volume, material. This approximates more to the operating characteristics of ordinary haulage vehicles, particularly since modern treatment and dumping sites are often at a considerable distance from gathering areas and entail lengthy main road journeys.

One of the very few concerns to consistently engage in making special purpose vehicles, while at the same time remaining consistently prosperous, is Scammell – and it is still the only part of the Leyland Vehicles group to do so, although it should be remembered that the company has always competed successfully in selling to ordinary road haulage, even if the vehicles themselves were often distinctly unconventional. It was in 1929 that the company achieved immortality with its first 100 tons capacity lorry, the magic century catching public imagination and lingering still in the folk-lore of people who care about such things. In truth 100 tons had long been well within the capacity of steam road locomotives produced by Fowler, McLaren, Aveling, and their contemporaries but the Scammell was petrol-engined, articulated, and clearly a herald of things to come.

For the next four decades, much encouraged by huge military contracts, the company designed and built its way into a dominant role in heavy

Above: If the variety of designs and operating modes still on offer is anything to go by, the problem of finding a universal transmission for heavy vehicles has yet to be solved. Certainly it was a major stumbling block for the first twenty years or so of vehicle development, and of the many ideas tried one of the few to have merit was the petrol-electric, in which an ordinary engine, coupled to a dynamo, supplied current to a traction motor. Control was easy, and acceleration could be smooth and surge-free. Leyland Motors did not do much toward petrol-electric development, but this example was built during 1909 – and predictably proved well suited to powering also a searchlight.

Left: Not what it seems, for despite the unmistakeably Leyland cab the chassis is an AEC – and was once a double-decked Regent. In general it may be said that buses lead more predictable and perhaps better serviced lives than do lorries. If, therefore, a use can be found for a time-expired bus it may well be able to give long trouble-free service in a quite new guise. Unfortunately the virtual passing of front-engined, drop-framed bus chassis has removed the most useful kind of vehicle, but while they lasted many users, needing a low height loading deck for their transport, used old buses. This one was put to work on road surface repairs.

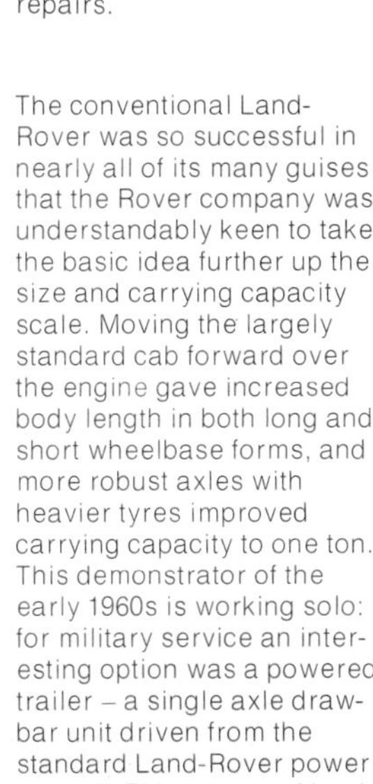

The conventional Land-Rover was so successful in nearly all of its many guises that the Rover company was understandably keen to take the basic idea further up the size and carrying capacity scale. Moving the largely standard cab forward over the engine gave increased body length in both long and short wheelbase forms, and more robust axles with heavier tyres improved carrying capacity to one ton. This demonstrator of the early 1960s is working solo: for military service an interesting option was a powered trailer – a single axle drawbar unit driven from the standard Land-Rover power take-off. This increased load capacity without reducing cross-country capability.

30
VIA ALBERT BRIDGE
ENJOY PHOENIX EXPORT PRIZE ALE

Heavy traffic meant most British trolley buses were double-decked, and many were six-wheeled too. This AEC in Belfast shows the style adopted in the mid-1930s.

Below: Heavy haulage specialists Pickfords, in the mid-1930s, sought a vehicle capable of carrying indivisible loads up to 18 tons, but wanted to avoid semi-trailers, knock-out axles, and the like. The result was built by AEC using Renown axles and powered by a diesel engine. In place of a conventional high level straight chassis the machinery carriers – three were made – had purpose made cranked frames welded up from rolled steel channel. The overall length was 30 ft. Quite apart from bus chassis on to which goods carrying bodywork is fitted, bus components have sometimes been used for other vehicles: notable were AEC and Leyland fire engines.

Civilian users would be foolish to allow their vehicles regularly to traverse ground as rough as this (**right**) – it would be more economic to prepare proper haul roads – but military authorities have to countenance any possibility. Scammell has long been willing to join such exercises and, as this early 1950s Meadows-engined Malayan oilfields vehicle shows, rough ground has to be very rough indeed before all-wheel drive, properly applied, is foiled. Under stimulus from the army Albion too has tried its hand at cross-country transport, and the amount of rear-axle articulation provided in this six-wheeler (**left**) is notable: so is the level chassis.

Below right: Every fleet engineer dreams of the ideal vehicle, but few are able to turn dream into reality. Such an opportunity came about during the 1950s within the then state controlled British Road Services. In addition to taking a hand in the development of the Bristol lorries (see page 67), BRS also decided it needed a purpose-built van for parcels delivery. Essentially the vehicles were standard BMCs of Austin descent, but the front end was restyled to provide excellent engine accessibility. Deep windscreens gave close-up visibility, and the drivers had hands-free walk-in cabs. Flat body sides made panel repair simple, too. Many were made over a 20-years span, and all were affectionately known as Noddy vans.

Right: Carrimore Six-Wheelers was a company which for many years concentrated upon drawbar and later semi-trailers, although at one period during the 1920s it dabbled with an urban delivery chassis. As the decade ended it also persuaded Leyland Motors to collaborate in a most out of character venture, in which what appeared to be virtually standard Leyland tractor units were sold complete with semi-trailers as plain Carrimores. They even had a Leyland-style model name, Lynx, although there was little in common with the later, lighter, Lynx. This Carrimore Lynx has pneumatic tyres: earlier ones were on solids, long after Leyland had apparently abandoned solids for such a vehicle.

Left: Perhaps it is not altogether surprising that Thornycrofts chose rear-steering for their first venture into motor transport, for it would be convenient to have the machinery near the crew, and easier to transmit steering effort, rather than drive, to the rear wheels. But as drivers on other kinds of vehicles have since found, rear-steer makes it difficult to maintain straight-line stability – and to control rear-end sideswing. Sculpture was another interest of the family, and this (still surviving) vehicle shared studio space during 1896 with the monument to Boadicea which now stands at the end of Westminster Bridge, in London.

Above: Articulation for buses can take either of two forms: one is now generally accepted in most parts of the world (illustrated on page 140); and the other is what amounts to a simple imitation of goods haulage practice. Never common, the latter scheme has usually been frowned on by authority, fearing instability on the road, and very few indeed have been built as double deckers. This example entered service in India during the late 1960s; the tractor unit was a Comet built by Ashok Leyland. Many, many Comets for goods and – conventional – bus work have emerged from the Indian Leyland company, but few have had the capacity of this 100-seater.

With the invaluable help of hindsight it seems now that the gas turbine era was no more than an interesting experimental interlude. Yet when in 1968 Leyland announced its gas turbine freight chassis it marked the culmination of two decades or more of development work by Rover into suitable engines, and it really did seem that the days of the big diesel were numbered. Apart from test rigs, six of these tractor units were made and put into service by potential buyers. There were some teething problems but generally they were reliable – however, by then diesel technology had moved on again, as it has a habit of doing. Gas turbines have yet to take the great leap forward which will put them in an unassailable position.

Right: The Bristol Lodekka gave low overall height with conventional interior: later versions had a forward entrance and stairs as on this United Automobile Services example at Scarborough.

Below: Leyland Motors adapted its standard body style in order to secure a part of the post-1945 orders for London buses. This batch were 8 ft wide – an innovation.

Opposite top: Before it began the rear-engined revolution Leyland Motors produced straightforward chassis designs, often carrying bodywork built by the company.

Opposite bottom: The great AEC venture into novelty was the Q-type of the 1930s. Its power unit was mounted in line behind the driver; most were single deckers.

WIGAN CORPORATION

DUNDALK
AU 337
ZY 1165

One notable omission from the Leyland Motor Corporation product line-up of the 1960s was a light, tough, four-wheel-drive chassis with which to compete for military, and particularly civilian, contracts. Developing such a machine was a task well suited to Scammell skills, and by dint of careful rearranging of standard components already in use within the group an apparently successful chassis was produced. Indeed there were two designs: this Chieftain Super Six, based on Albion components, and a very similar version which used Leyland Comet units. In the event the whole idea was dropped until, much later, a purpose-built four by four emerged which was based on the BMC-Leyland Redline chassis.

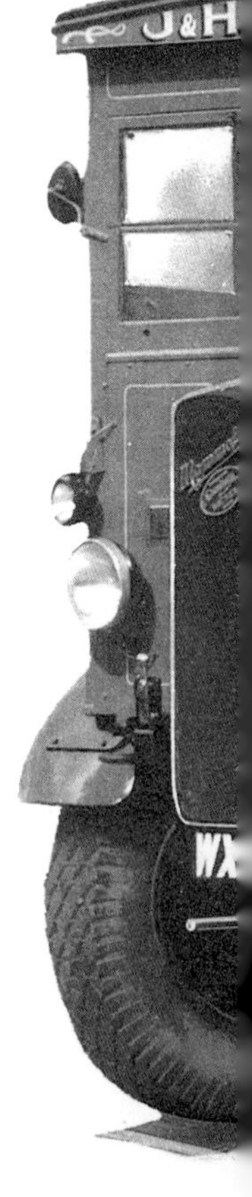

Above: Leyland, no doubt eyeing the progress in bus design being made in America, Germany, and elsewhere, began trials in 1936 of a rear-engined chassis. It had a transverse diesel engine and transmission driving forward to the rear axle, and thus aped contemporary American production models while anticipating what has become the standard layout for British double deckers. The bodywork, incidentally, was largely the top half of a double decker. Not much came of this essay, but a year or two later collaboration with London produced a fleet of underfloor and integral construction single deckers, followed by some with their power units at the rear, but mounted in line with the chassis.

Right: AEC was a pioneer, in Britain, of diesel engines designed specifically for road vehicles, and in close collaboration with its then sister organisation the London General Omnibus Company made rapid progress. Throughout its lifespan the company usually had available engines to match whatever need was in hand; on the rare occasions when a customer insisted on rival power units being used, the fact was kept quiet if possible. Yet this Mammoth, photographed in 1933, has on its radiator grille an elliptical 'Gardner diesel' badge; it had, in fact, been converted from petrol by an agency not far from the owner's address, and no doubt the resulting saving in fuel bills was much appreciated.

haulage of all kinds and notably in oilfields exploration and exploitation. Such work led naturally into building off-road dump trucks, but although many were made they competed neither in size nor numbers with the firms, particularly those of American origin, specialising in civil engineering plant. Aveling Barford, not a member of the modern Leyland Vehicles but the one plant specialist in BL, also kept away from the very largest carriers.

While lorrymen, on the whole, prefer convention the nature of bus work is such as to positively encourage unconventional designs that rapidly become convention. Engines under the floor and at the rear were startling innovations that soon became commonplace, but it was notable that attempts to transfer technology from passenger carrying to freight transport failed signally, although Albion tried hard for a few years in the 1950s and 1960s with underfloor-engined chassis which seemed ideal for delivery and parcels work. Almost inevitably Leyland tried a rear-engined lorry chassis, an eight-wheeler intended for tanker work, but it attracted no buyers. Integral construction, common in passenger work and which might be thought well suited to many kinds of modern lorry, has likewise failed to make the transition – except in the limited sense that many Scammell-built semi-trailer tankers were self-supporting and frameless, together with some designs of semi-trailer box vans.

Unconventional power units have never appealed to users and the only exception so far is that of the diesel engine which gained acceptance so rapidly that it soon became convention personified. So much so that the handful of Leyland lorries built with Rover-produced gas turbine engines remain curiosities, although at their introduction in 1968 it was confidently predicted that the new form of power source would soon replace diesel.

At first sight it is curious that the diesel revolution, virtually complete by 1950 amongst British heavy vehicles of all kinds, still has far to go among lightweights, for it is only in very recent years that oil engines have achieved the status of so much as optional equipment in sales brochures. On closer investigation it is less surprising, for apart from largely unfounded suspicion of diesels on the part of potential buyers the mileage covered during the lifespans of many light vans and trucks is too low to justify the significantly higher first cost entailed by expensive fuel injection equipment, more powerful starting equipment, and generally more robust structure. Not only does the money saved initially buy a great deal of petrol but the owners of one, two, or three vehicle 'fleets' will probably feel more confident in the ownership of vehicles which are mechanically much like their family cars.

But if tradition is still evident in their power units all makers of the lightest vehicles so thoroughly abandoned the old ways in the general construction of their products that they form another example of great and dangerous novelty becoming the unquestioned norm. The close links between mass-produced passenger cars and vans (and the trucks derived from them) successfully survived the great leap to pressed steel and integral construction from pieced together bodywork based on chassis frames, as well as from the days when commercial vehicle production on these chassis was almost an afterthought. This led to such fundamentally unsatisfactory oddities as the BSA Scout van of the 1930s, a three-wheeler with its single rear wheel under the load.

464 LYNEHAM
WHW 373H

The Bristol RE was a neat and workmanlike design which bypassed many of the problems afflicting other rear-engined designs with an unusual drive line.

There could, of course, also be happier outcomes like the MG Midget service van – and it is worth recalling that one of the strangest of unconventionals, the Trojan, which in its formative years was owned by Leyland Motors, met small success in its original role as a passenger car but went on to acceptance as an economical and reliable light van with a secure market niche all its own. In more recent times van and truck bodywork left its origins completely and came to be designed into projected product ranges along with the saloon, estate, and hatchback versions. The inevitable result was that an overall 'car look' came to characterise light commercials, which generally lost much of the visible evidence of their small lorry origins. Among British makers notable leads in this direction were given in the post-war years by Austin, with its A40 and A70 families, and Standard, with its Vanguards and Ensigns. Morris vans and pick-ups, particularly the long-lived Minor range, were much more in the traditional style of noticeably separate bodies on chassis but were not the less commercially successful for that. Indeed, the British postal authorities liked them so much that they continued to buy Minor vans long after they were no longer available to the general public.

Austin persevered with its good-looking des-

cendants of the A40; the Marina of the 1970s owed more of its appearance to Longbridge than to Cowley. Van versions of the Metro have no forebears, and indeed are hardly more than cars with the rearmost window openings panelled over. Front-wheel drive has come a long way since the BSA Scout.

The integral range, if not integral construction, approach took Standard into a van version of its Herald car which, too, was not much more than an estate without windows, but despite its slim good looks it soon succumbed under Leyland ownership. More successful was the Standard Atlas, a factory-made panel van in what was already a well-established idiom elsewhere in the world. Austin-Morris was in the market with a van (and a few pick-ups as well) derived jointly from the

Left: As the production and use of 'mains' electricity spread through Britain, power stations looked hard for off-peak loading. An obvious source was battery-electric vehicles which could be recharged – at favourable prices – during slack hours. So the 1920s and 1930s saw many electric fleets in use. Since power generation was often in the hands of local government authorities it followed that their own transport could be electric, and Guy was one of several firms to produce battery-powered vehicles for municipal use. This side-loading refuse collector was made during 1922; Guy soon lost interest in battery power, and so did most of its rivals.

Above: Despite many false dawns, battery-electric traction has yet to make the impact on road transport which its supporters have so fervently desired. A telling illustration of the way in which hopes have so often been dashed is the frequency and complexity of new foundings and regroupings among manufacturers. Morrison, which made this 2-tons capacity machine in 1952, was (in one form or another) a long-lived concern and for some years it was the property of Austin, and thence BMC and BLMC. Battery weight is the great drawback to this seemingly attractive means of propulsion and payload can be almost unimportant compared with unladen weight.

Below: While one Crossley department was struggling hard to win and hold a toe-hold in the bus business, another was managing very much better in the somewhat more sheltered world of military equipment. Soon after the end of the First World War, the British government began to form a new set of subvention chassis specifications, and it was inevitable that pneumatic tyres would be included. Crossley produced a wide range of military and military specification models, including this six-wheeled load carrier for the Indian Army in 1930: the cranked chassis provided extra clearance for the double-drive rear bogie to articulate on rough ground.

Private
WEST MON OMNIBUS BOARD

From the mid-1950s on, the standard British single decker had its engine mounted under the floor. The Leyland Tiger Cub was typical, and had a long life.

Above: Soaring fuel costs have led, since the early 1970s, to intensive and sustained research into reducing consumption by vehicles – in which fuel prices are a dominant aspect of operating overheads. Much has been done, and much more will be done, to improve the fuel efficiency of engines; something can also be done with running gear – although it must be said that driver education could be the most productive of all. Useful savings can result from paying attention to the external form. Comparative trials show that air deflectors, as fitted to this Terrier cab roof, and other minor panelling additions designed to smooth air flow over the vehicle, can be well worthwhile.

Below: The oil crisis of the mid-1970s led to renewed experimenting with forms of power other than internal combustion. The state-owned National Bus Company wished to be seen participating in this movement and so put into service a battery-powered, but otherwise largely standard, National bus. Like most electric vehicles it worked satisfactorily, but unfortunately novelty stopped at its trailerful of batteries, which were of conventional lead-acid type. Even under favourable conditions on a bus-only route overall performance was hardly better than that achieved by battery vehicles over 90 years: an operating range of about 60 miles at contemporary road speeds.

stylish Morris J of the 1950s and the much larger and in its day distinctly original Austin three-way, which combined a spacious body with a door in each side and one at the rear. Such mechanical novelty as all these possessed lay in the engine position, which was between or under the cab seats and thereby imitated competitors. It was noticeable that when Leyland group policy for this class of vehicle was reformulated, with the intention of producing a thoroughly practical machine low in cost of production and of ownership, the resulting Sherpa abandoned all novelty and had its power unit housed under a protruding bonnet at the front, where engines have so often been placed during the last eighty years; the body became a simple and straightforward box. Both rear-mounted engines, and front-wheel drive, either of which for different reasons might have appealed to company designers were eschewed in favour of conventional simplicity.

Meanwhile the novelty of factory made and integral construction has continued to move steadily up the weight range although it has to be said that for sufficiently powerful reasons the Leyland group companies lagged well behind rival concerns in moving to higher capacities. There was once, it is true, the handsome and effective Austin-Morris LD range of vans which Leyland Motors sought to rival with its model 90, an extraordinary confection of Standard engine, Rootes Group gearbox, BMC rear axle, and the Leyland, Albion, Dodge, cab. The 90 could not be termed a commercial success, and nor really was the EA (although much longer lived), spawned by BMC, revised by BLMC, and finally replaced by larger and well thought out versions of the Sherpa. These newest light commercials are from the Freight Rover part of BL, but form a downward extension of the commercial vehicle range, which is now as comprehensive as its competitors.

Railcars

The Newcomer

There was a great deal of pressure on British Railways, during the years when steam was finally giving way, for it to experiment with light railbuses on what might be termed the quietest branch lines. BR spread its net widely and bought railbuses from a variety of suppliers including Bristol-ECW and Park Royal – the latter had earlier built a consider-able number of full-sized conventional units for Ireland. This is a Park Royal car (**below**) at work in Scotland. The wheel turned almost full circle, in the full-ness of time, when Leyland began to experiment with its National bus body pressings, producing a modern railbus that is mounted on a four-wheeled wagon under-frame originally developed for operation in fast goods trains. This early sample (**bottom**) of British Rail Engineering-Leyland co-operation still wears a 'National 2' bus badge.

For economical running under all conditions
Railway undertakings can rely upon

A.E.C.
DIESEL RAILCARS

A.E.C. Limited, Southall, Middlesex, is a member of the Group of Companies controlled by Associated Commercial Vehicles Ltd., of which the selling organisation is

A.C.V. SALES LTD., 49 BERKELEY SQUARE, LONDON, W.1. Telephone: REGENT 2141

Above: After 1945 AEC, Leyland, and Albion engines were used in a large number of diesel multiple-unit trains supplied through BUT to British Railways. Underframes and bodies were built by a variety of railway makers, including Pressed Steel, which is perhaps better known as a member of British Motor Holdings and a maker of car bodywork. Pressed Steel also produced a number of single-unit railcars, that is with a driving cab at each end, for use on smaller branch lines. This one was in the 1980s working on the Windsor branch, but with another conventional driving unit coupled at its other end. The twin exhaust pipes running up to roof level are the recognition point of these single-unit cars.

Preceding pages: BUT was heavily involved in providing power packs for diesel multiple unit trains for British Railways, with Albion, AEC and Leyland engines. Car bodybuilders Pressed Steel built this common single unit example, seen at Looe. **Insert:** A search for extra work for the Workington Leyland National plant led to the railbus, based on a British Rail engineering-built underframe. This is the third prototype at Sea Mills near Bristol.

Leyland Motors also interested itself in applying road vehicle techniques to railway applications, an added incentive being its Lysholm-Smith fluid transmission, of use in buses but with even greater potential in diesel railway traction. Railways on the home market, notably the London Midland and Scottish, were interested and tried Leyland products, but the company cast its net wider. This motor car-trailer set (**bottom**) was put to work in Australia, where difficulties in guaranteeing a regular and suitable water supply added to the enthusiasm of railway officials keen to lessen dependence on steam. The power bogie (**below**) was one of six sets for New Zealand, and illustrates graphically the great limitations on space under the floors of rail vehicles – particularly those used on narrow guage systems, like New Zealand.

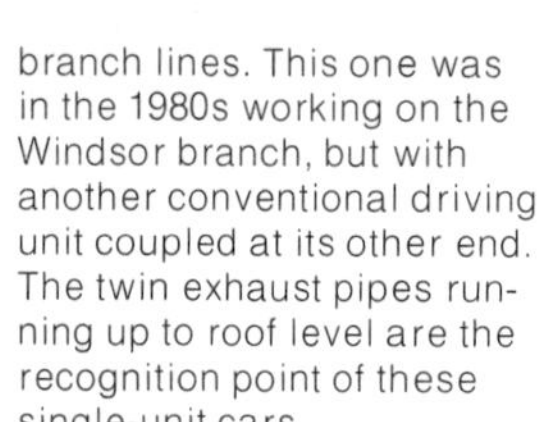

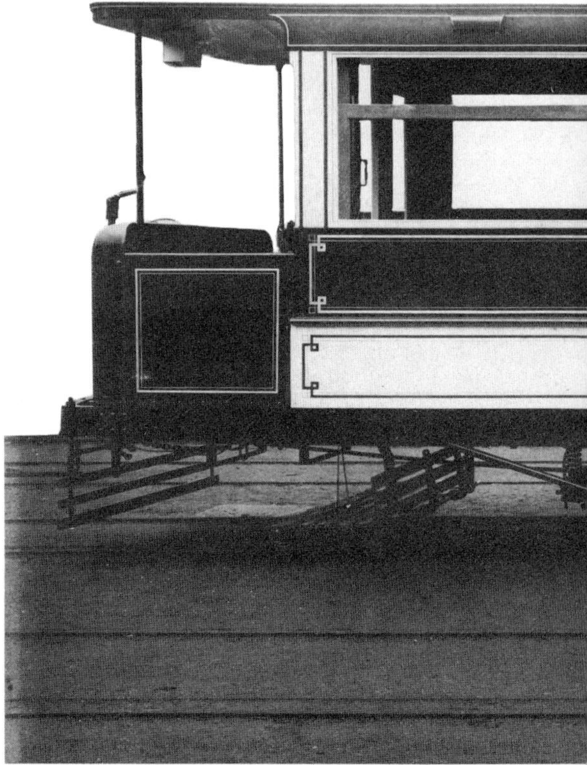

On the 'Streamline Great Western'

A pronounced advance in design, it is natural that the 'Streamline Great Western' should have Timken tapered roller bearings.

Timken tapered roller bearings, by their great capacity for journal and thrust loads, greatly reduce frictional losses, especially starting effort.

Incorporating the results of many years' experience on high duty bearings and employing the best workmanship and materials, they lower maintenance cost to the absolute minimum, avoiding all those troubles common to the ordinary plain bearing.

Each Great Western A.E.C. Diesel Railcar has five Timken axle boxes.

BRITISH TIMKEN LTD., CHESTON ROAD, ASTON, BIRMINGHAM

A typical Timken axle box.

TIMKEN TAPERED ROLLER BEARINGS

By the 1930s railway administrations in many parts of the world were becoming seriously worried about the low efficiency and high costs of steam-hauled carriages and the loss of traffic to road transport. For many of their applications something less costly and more flexible was required. Naturally they turned to road transport technology, for by then the diesel engine had undoubtedly come to stay. The Great Western Railway in Britain was an internal combustion railcar pioneer having tried an early petrol unit (**above**), powered by a Maudslay engine. Then during the 1930s it built up a considerable fleet of these AEC railcars (**left**), all futuristically styled, and some of them able to run in multiple.

Combination Train, Derwent Valley Railway.
Built by Messrs. Charles H. Roe (1923) Ltd.

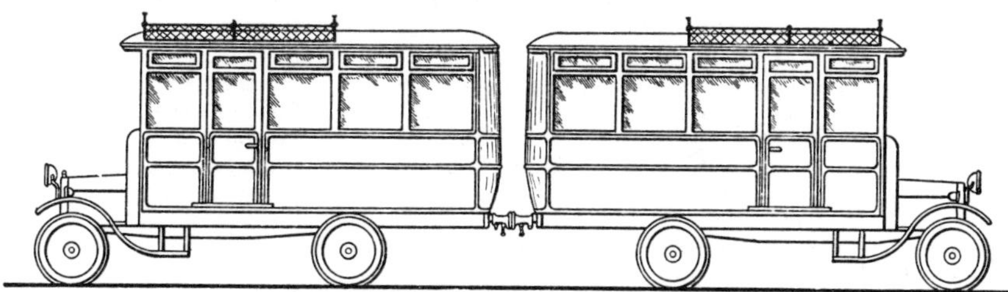

Elevation of Combination Train.

One of the best known – but sadly least photographed – ventures by Leyland into rail transport was the small batch of petrol-powered tramcars made for use in Morecambe (**left**). Like all regular trams they could be driven from either end, and they were fitted with four-speed gearboxes. Like the few others of their kind, petrol, and later diesel, power and street tramways proved to be incompatible; the same must also be said of attempts to place road vehicles on to rails. The stresses of the one mode are quite different to those of the other, and road vehicles soon break up when steel tyres replace those of rubber. However, during the mid-1920s, as the Morecambe tram bowed out, Roe produced this twin railbus set (**above**) for the little Derwent Valley Railway. Propulsion problems were minimised by driving only the car which was leading: the other trailed.

The Third World minibuses generally known as jeepneys were not often based on Land-Rover chassis, but local enterprise in Borneo produced a sturdy vehicle.

LAXANG ROAD BUS CO.LTD.
SIBU, SARAWAK
10 PASSENGERS SEATED
TON CWTS QRS LBS
Nº 1   9   0   24
Gt 2   14   0   24
DRINK
Coca-Cola

Selling abroad

When the somewhat hysterical exhortation to 'export or die' became a British political catch-phrase of the late 1940s many members of the motor industry no doubt looked at each other and drew deep breaths of exasperation. They had been exporting rather than dying for decades and knew far, far more than any of those who sought to goad them about the difficulties and often thin rewards of that hazardous means of earning a living.

The vehicles they had to sell had become nearly as good as any made by rivals in other countries, and in some respects were well in advance. The heavy chassis makers, for example, were producing acceptable oil-engined vehicles long before most of their foreign competitors, while British trolley bus builders, led by AEC and Guy, were well ahead of the field. When, after a few rosy post-1945 years, by the mid-1960s, a trading gap opened and widened it was largely the result of events over which British vehicle makers had no control, although they had often sought to change them.

Quite the most important consideration in selling overseas, most had found, was that any success was inextricably intertwined with success at home: overseas markets were a source of added sales, but profit margins there were tight; the money came from customers at home where conditions were easier and sometimes more predictable. But each outlet was viable only in the context of the volume of sales it added to the total. Lose too much of either and the whole business was in jeopardy.

Unfortunately, while many other countries progressively eased their domestic restrictions on vehicle design and use, Britain lagged behind.

The reasons no doubt seemed sound at the time and are now immaterial but during the early 1930s, when America built a coast-to-coast road system which fostered profitable journeys of enormous length, and France and Germany were encouraging heavy commercial vehicles to run at 50 mph or more, similar equipment in Britain would have been limited to a plodding 20 mph – 30 mph for lightweights. These and equally restrictive limits on vehicle dimensions inevitably stunted the growth of operators who saw no reason to buy chassis built to specifications any higher than the bare minimum. Lorries able to earn a living for their owners on winding and narrow British roads were hopelessly under-powered and underbraked on the new wide, straight, motor roads that were being constructed elsewhere. This was unimportant in the railway-orientated 1920s and 1930s, but by 1950 the world was running on pneumatic tyres, and although for another two decades British bus builders held their own, truck markets inevitably began to look at other than British products. It should also be observed that for ten years after the war ended both the manufacturing and operating sides of the road transport business in Britain suffered frequent and erratic political interventions which undermined any real attempts at forward planning, either financial or technical.

Certainly the late flowering in Britain of the motorway age from 1959 on, coupled with a more congenial economic climate, brought rapid revisions of thought. Soon there appeared home produced designs well able to meet operator demands created by a steadily growing network of modern roads coupled with belated relaxation of vehicle weights and dimensions legislation. It

A bus with a difference. The semi-trailer coupled to this Scammel Mountaineer could seat up to 126 people. The sand tyres indicate that it was destined for desert use, and while it is hard to envisage any circumstances in which such a tractor would be needed solely for passenger work, it would form a convenient way of transporting a labour force to and from a worksite – where the tractor could then spend its days engaged in duties more suited to its abilities. The Scammell Mountaineer was generally available in two basic forms – as a dump truck with a gross weight of 24 tons, or as an articulated tractor the largest of which could haul up to 60 tons gross.

was, however, too late for many members of a heavily fragmented manufacturing industry. As individuals they were unable to compete because of the sheer impossibility of raising enough money to develop whole new ranges of products capable of winning and holding worthwhile shares of the home market – and also of selling abroad against the newly rejuvenated and very aggressive motor manufacturers of France, Italy, Germany, and America. There were growing threats too from places before hardly considered, including Sweden, Spain, and Holland; nor had it escaped the notice of financial institutions standing behind the British motor industry that in too

Above left: The British government revived its subvention scheme during the 1920s, and many manufacturers produced vehicles which matched the specifications laid down. But, unlike pre-1914 designs, which led to chassis that could be used for goods or passenger work, military or civilian, the later scheme created vehicles which were essentially military in character and less suitable generally for civilian users. However, machines of this kind were ideal for developing countries, and many were shipped overseas. More than 300 of these Albion six-wheelers of 3 tons capacity were bought by the government of India during the 1930s.

Above right: So rapid was the course of events that only one original commercial vehicle design came from Standard Triumph following its acquisition by Leyland. 'Original' is something of a misnomer, for the Leyland 2-tonner turned out to be an amalgam of an extraordinary collection of components, adorned by another version of the LAD cab. The vehicle was not much of a success and failed to survive the LMC-BMH merger, but while it lasted efforts were made to sell it in all the then strong Leyland markets overseas. This one went to Greece, which country also took that other Standard Triumph product, the Leyland 20 – which had started as the Standard Atlas.

Left: The curious case of the exports that stayed at home in order to go abroad. The notorious case of the chassisless Leyland Olympic buses destined for Cuba, but which sank instead to the bottom of the Thames estuary after the ship carrying them collided with another, is well known. That was in 1964. Less well known is that some of the vehicles lived to run again. Among them was a pair which were reconditioned and received Van Hool bodywork. In this new guise they went into service with a British tours operator on his Continental itineraries, where of course their left-hand drive proved most useful. Others, incidentally, were converted into vans.

Bottom: The Utic concern, originally formed by an association of Portuguese coach operators, was another of the considerable number of European builders to use British origin components. During the early 1970s the company was taking AEC Swift power units and running gear and building them into its own design of integral coach, using welded steel tube for the load bearing frame. The Swift connexion lasted until the end of AEC in 1979, but the company first began collaborating with AEC during the mid-1950s. Indeed in 1960 a joint production facility was started. The bus on the left has its panels and mouldings being fixed; the spectral vehicle on the right is in the throes of being painted.

Following pages: The model name Freighter covers all the medium and heavyweight four-wheelers, introduced by Leyland Vehicles to replace chassis of Albion and BMC origin.

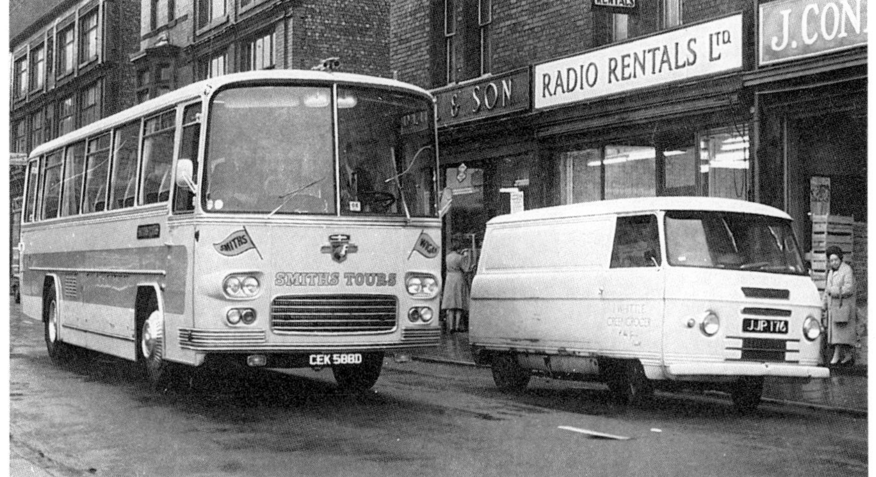

NEW 11-16 TONNE FREIGHTERS
LEYLAND
FREIGHTER
FREIGHTER

MULDER
MULDER
M 3³
13-11

Left: The range of lorries introduced early in the 1930s by Crossley was intended, with its contemporary buses, to give the company a firmer foothold in the new world of diesel-engined vehicles. Although they failed, instead becoming heavily involved with military work, during the five or six years that production lasted, the distinctive front end of the Crossley goods vehicles was to be seen on the road. This Delta of 1934 went to Mauritius, and it shows the curious bus-style front wings and set back radiator of its kind. Most Crossleys were forward control, but the Delta could also be had with a bonneted layout.

From its earliest days the Thornycroft road vehicle business benefited from the worldwide perspective of its shipbuilding parent. By the 1930s there were wholly-owned subsidiary companies in both Sydney and Melbourne, Australia; Wellington, New Zealand; Singapore; Egypt; the Argentine; and the biggest of all in Rio de Janeiro and Sao Paulo, Brazil. Elsewhere there were plenty of agents. The single-decked bus (**below**) was one of a fleet of 140 delivered to Egypt in the early 1930s; the transit mixer (**right**) went to Australia in 1955. It was a Trusty built to export specification for gross loads of 21 tons. By this time Thornycroft was sending overseas about half its production, and its home market position was dangerously weakened.

For some classes of work, motor vehicles are at a distinct disadvantage compared with horse transport – someone must be at the wheel before they can move. Hence the outside steering wheel of this 1951 Morris-Commercial, which went to the Netherlands municipality of Bunschoten. Conventional door-to-door refuse collection is in manpower terms an expensive business; when the first moves were made towards mechanical transport, several vehicle makers offered the option of kerbside control, with low speed crawler gears and steering. Parked cars and modern traffic generally make such ideas quite impractical today.

There is, of course, no means of telling what was in the crates and hampers 'Not Wanted on the Voyage', but this New Zealand Albion of about 1911 certainly appears to be carrying more than its rated capacity of 30 cwt. Albion was a cautious concern, and did not change models or details until there was good reason: hence the chain final drive shown on this example stayed in the Albion range much longer than it did with other successful makers. And the products were sufficiently robust for there to be no need for special export models. The resulting combination of simplicity, reliability and reasonable price gave the company worthwhile markets in many overseas countries.

Following pages: For the important civil engineering industry Leyland Vehicles offers two basic Constructors – six and eight-wheeled. Both are assembled from standard components.

Originally Austin was largely concerned with better quality passenger cars, but from early in the company's history it showed an interest in taxicab work. For this purpose a compact vehicle was, and is, desirable and Austin achieved this by positioning the driver over the engine. It followed that similar chassis were well suited to urban delivery vans too, and a fair number were sold for both purposes before 1914. This Austin van was exported in 1913 to the Brazilian postal authority: it differed hardly at all – apart from engine details – from those of five years earlier. For this model Austin placed the steering column centrally, an unusual feature.

LEYLAND
CONSTRUCTOR
24·21

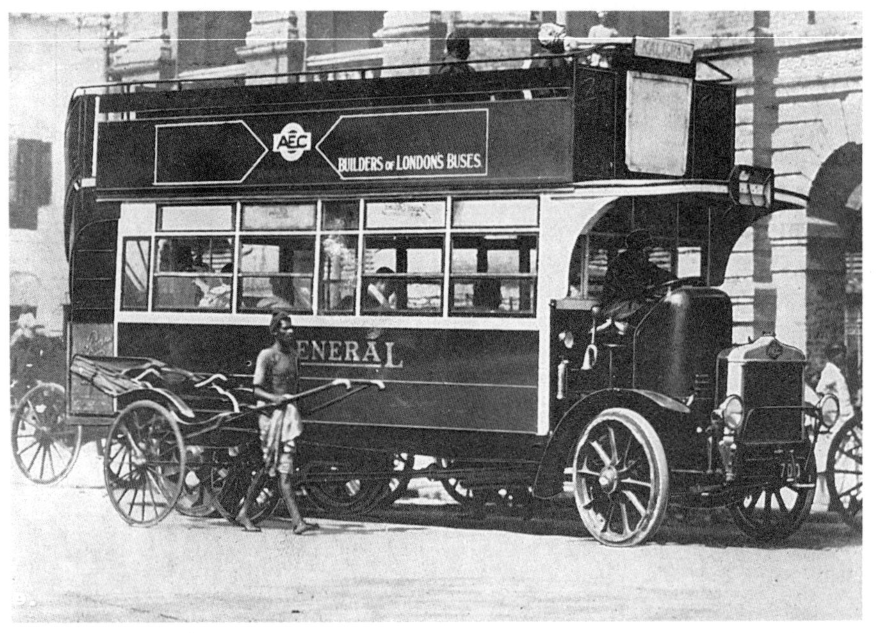

The sizeable lead in urban bus operating methods built up by the main London undertakings – buttressed as they were by AEC – created a respect for, and a desire to emulate, many things from London, particularly the vehicles themselves. Virtually standard London buses were sent not only all over Britain but also to, among other places, Buenos Aires, Vienna, Berlin, and even Pittsburgh. The Regent about to be swung on board ship (**right**) was on its way to Stockholm in about 1930, but instead it could have joined the London General Omnibus ST fleet without causing comment. The S-type in Calcutta (**left**) during 1924 is completely London, not only to the fleet name but also in its destination display.

many overseas markets competition had traditionally come from rival British factories.

This awkward state of affairs was in large part a result of British history. Even without such assistance as widespread financial inducements to trade with the home country it was inevitable that administrators of the British Empire would be inclined to buy wherever possible from their homeland, and equally inevitable that manufacturers in Britain would prefer to trade in countries where the political climate was comfortable. Such trading began early – indeed, long before petrol engines, and much steam-powered agricultural and industrial plant made by an-

cestors of the present BL group went overseas. Later, and considering the fragility of early motor vehicles, outposts of the Empire showed considerable enterprise by buying such machines and somehow keeping them running.

Despite such precocious efforts the real stimulus to the growth of motor transport throughout the world was the First World War – more precisely, the advanced and reliable vehicles that resulted from wartime development and also the considerable reserves of men trained by armies in motor skills. A great help was, of course, that lorries made at that time were built to withstand battlefield conditions, and so the lack in most

The Leyland companies worked hard in their trade with Africa, and throughout the 1950s and 1960s were quite prepared to build what the customers wanted. In an example of local enterprise by Leyland Albion (Africa), the South African company produced in 1958 this Voortrekker (**centre**), a tough four-wheeled bus with two-pedal control and the ability to cope with poor roads or hardly any roads at all. Machines for these very difficult operating conditions were good business for several British factories, and in both four and six-wheeled forms (**bottom**). AEC and, notably, Guy, sold many, and sometimes the chassis were fitted with bodywork (**right**) that was half passenger, half goods.

countries outside Europe of anything deserving of the name road was not as serious a handicap as might have been thought. In any case, as soon as lorries proved themselves to be indispensable then highways came along soon enough to carry them. British factories were further aided, once the war was over, by the continued interest of Empire governments in vehicles suitable for military use in their own countries. By definition such machinery was also perfectly suited to civilian purposes in the Australian outback or South African veldt.

For many years, apart from a handful of exceptions, the chassis of vehicles made in Britain for sale abroad were similar to those made for sale at home. At least the components from which they were assembled were the same, and while this state of affairs was perfectly acceptable for the first four decades of motors the freedom to increase vehicle sizes and speeds that came with pneumatic tyres led users in such places as Australia, South Africa, and the Middle East to demand something bigger and faster than before.

Increasingly in such places Britain became only one of several suppliers. Canada, heavily dominated by the American motor industry, had a ready source of such equipment and despite noble efforts, particularly by Leyland Motors,

Britain rapidly lost the small hold it had in North American markets. Happily in South America long-standing business connexions in Argentina, Uruguay, Venezuela, Chile, and other Latin states made easier the task of companies which sought to continue and expand the old reliance of those places on British transport expertise. Many a railway and tramway in South America had been built and financed – operated too, very often – by the British and this connexion helped AEC, Thornycroft, Leyland, Albion, and others to sell.

Then during the post-1945 years came developments nearer home which with hindsight could have been harbingers of a future that instead faded away. Broadly, the truly enormous overseas trade carried out by British commercial vehicle makers lay historically with countries that for one reason or another did not make comparable vehicles of their own, and therefore continental Europe did not figure prominently among the lists of customers. But the continental factories suffered terribly as the war reached its end and were quite incapable of meeting the demand for transport needed in wholesale national reconstruction, British plants, on the other hand, although badly affected were still capable of production and with that 'export or die' ringing in their ears sent every chassis that could be spared and many that could not on to the roads of friends and erstwhile enemies.

In such circumstances anything could be sold, new or secondhand, but as local factories got themselves back into production the demand for lorries tended to fall away. Bus economics are framed in longer time scales and so it was that the sales between 1945 and 1950 created European links which lasted until commercial enterprise in the Leyland Group was fatally distracted by the internal company woes of the 1970s. For years Stockholm depended heavily on Leyland buses; Crossley sold many, including a fleet of unusual articulated vehicles, to the Netherlands railways; the major Dutch cities depended upon Leyland, AEC, and Guy products; Madrid and Lisbon rode on AECs and Leylands; and Spanish tourists often travelled in Guys. Oslo bought Daimlers, and Leylands. Local builders and assemblers relied on major components, largely from Leyland and AEC. Kromhout and Verheul (also an AEC assembler) built the Royal Holland integral with Royal Tiger sub-assemblies; the Swedish railways built integrals using Leyland and Albion components; the Italian Viberti made articulated buses with Leyland parts. There were many such, and perhaps as many again, partnerships with local companies.

After a successful joint contract to supply Poland, Leyland took an interest in DAB of Denmark. The French Willeme allied itself to AEC and the Austin-Morris division of BMC. Utic in Portugal used Leyland and AEC components in a successful range of vehicles, and so did the Finnish Sisu and Vanaja companies. In Spain Barreiros joined AEC while Pegaso built Leyland engines under licence. So did the Dutch DAF company, Scania in Sweden, Sisu in Finland, and in Poland the WSK factory. Indeed despite continuing successes by others it had become clear

by 1960 that AEC and Leyland were going to outstrip all other British chassis makers in the race for continental Europe. If earlier attempts had succeeded in forming a European Economic Community which also included Britain then not the least of the beneficiaries may well have been the motor industry – for specialist engine and other component makers had built up considerable trading relationships, in particular with what were to become the BL companies.

Instead the rapid drawing together of the founding six members effectively shut out British manufacturers, and considerably weakened their position in the non-EEC European countries as well. They reconcentrated their attentions on the wider world, and when finally membership of the Common Market club was conceded the companies found themselves, as one of the incidental conditions of entry, excluded by newly raised tariff and customs barriers from colonial markets that had long been largely their own preserves. As compensation they were admitted instead to countries already filled to overflowing with well-established local firms.

So it was hardly the fault of the manufacturers that many hitherto open doors worldwide were closed, or nearly so. But while they lasted the post-war exporting years were heady times. During the mid-1960s the Leyland-Albion-Scammell team could claim to be: 'The world's largest exporters of heavy duty vehicles', and no one disputed it. Between them they were supplying vehicles, parts, and service to about 130 countries. In 1964 BMC – still separate then – boasted that its 50-model commercial vehicle range in each of the Austin and Morris catalogues was the biggest in Europe. By 1965 it was said to be the biggest in the world.

A particularly far-sighted move by Leyland was to involve itself with factories jointly owned with local interests in India, Israel, Iran, and more recently Nigeria. While still subject to local economic buffetings these plants and those elsewhere that assemble vehicles from kits of parts do help to overcome the rapidly growing unwillingness of many countries to import complete vehicles when at least some of the content could be provided locally.

One of the bravest, or cheekiest, attempts to prise open a closed door was the sale during the early 1960s of a small fleet of Leyland-Albion tractors to a New York operator. In another unlikely enterprise Superior Coach of Ohio was sending kit-bodied AEC Reliances to Indonesia; by then Twin Coach, also of Ohio, had taken hundreds of Leyland diesels for installing as replacements for petrol units in American-made heavy vehicles, and International Harvester chose Austin petrol engines to power its Metro Mite delivery van. (There had been, in the 1930s, an American Austin company making Austin vans under licence.) In Canada some Comets, Bisons, and Beavers fitted with local cabs struggled to reforge links that had withered on the outbreak of war in 1939; meanwhile AEC was supplying engines to Canadian Car, and the Hayes concern in British Columbia built heavy lorries using Leyland parts. Daimler sold, in 1966, urban single

Left: The Dutch Verheul bodybuilding concern was a post-1945 success story, producing buses and coaches and fitting Leyland units into integrally-bodied vehicles. Then in 1960 the company was acquired by AEC and turned to AEC components: following the formation of the LMC, and some name changes, the firm became Leyland Verheul and again turned to Leyland for its running gear. Apart from becoming a dominant force in its home market – it took control of Kromhout, another Netherlands user of Leyland components – Verheul became an exporter. This single decker from the AEC days, lightly disguised as an ACLO, was destined for a customer in South America.

deckers to Edmonton and Calgary.

At one time and including re-engining work Leyland claimed to hold 92 per cent of the Canadian diesel engine market. Indeed the early perfecting of diesels in Britain, coupled with 'Imperial Preference' financing arrangements, made it possible for British makers to at least stay in the market against nominally cheaper American products, despite the heavy additional costs of transatlantic shipping. During the inter-war years the seemingly limitless scope for growth in Canada had led to several firms trying their fortunes there, from the little Austin Seven up to Crossley military specification chassis for the armed services. During those years AEC and Leyland conducted another of their interminable battles, this time in long-distance coaching.

The rapid development of Middle Eastern oil-fields during the immediate post-1945 period provided a golden age for Scammell and Thornycroft, both of which had the sort of facilities needed to design and produce specialised heavy transport and who sold the results to Ecuador, Burma, the Persian Gulf, Turkey, Rumania, and indeed to anywhere that the rigs were drilling. Scammell engineering gave the company a decided edge in 'go anywhere' vehicles able to carry or haul loads of many tons across territory where roads had yet to be thought of. For years the standard Scammell display at exhibitions included a three-axle machine of this kind, with its diagonally opposite wheels standing on blocks 18 in or so high. Thornycroft leaned towards highway tractors of gigantic proportions, and its Mighty Antar became an immortal, not least among the many armies that adopted it for battle tank transporting. But Thornycroft had long held thriving connexions in many territories where tough vehicles were needed and during the 1930s had supplied fleets of buses to Cairo, and Africa generally, in addition to robust 'on-highway' vehicles of all kinds. Sadly Thornycroft became an example of an exporter which also died: for too long about half its production went abroad abroad

There are two main draw-backs to the practice of exporting complete buses: shipping costs are high, and there is little work content in the vehicles for citizens of the receiving country. Both objections can be overcome by sending complete sets of parts from which buses can be assembled: all of the difficult work requiring expensive machinery is already done, but there are many man-hours of simple work in putting the vehicles together. Saunders thought hard about the possibilities of this scheme and by the early 1950s was able to offer a sound kit system, based on three chassis – in this case Leyland Worldmasters. The first carries three sets of roofs (**top**), the second three sets of side frames (**centre**), and the third (**bottom**) has the front and rear ends. Sundry components fill up the odd corners.

Above right: Enormous increases in population coupled with strictly limited road space presented the transport authorities in Hong Kong with an unenviable problem, to which the answer was at least in part seen as double decker buses. When new this Guy, belonging to China Motor Bus, was a single decker 'Long Dragon', 36 ft in over-all length, seating 29 passengers, and worked with a crew of five. The chassis was then shortened to 30 ft and fitted with an MCW double-decked body, imported from Britain, which had previously been carried by an AEC Regent. Now the vehicle is one-man operated. The Guy is not unique: many elderly front-engined chassis have been rebuilt for further use.

while the company steadily lost its place on the home market.

Until the rapid development of Japan in more recent times the countries of the Far East were so far away from any potential supplier of commercial vehicles that Britain, despite the huge distances involved, was as well placed as any to secure its share of trade – and, again, the old Imperial connexion was a great help. As long ago as the 1920s local officials in India were complaining that British makers were not producing vehicles sturdy enough or sufficiently adapted to meet local conditions. The warning was in large part heeded, but inevitably independent India sought independence in its vehicle supplies also. Most of its needs now are met by home factories – even if they are operating largely under licences from other countries, of which the successful Ashok Leyland arrangement, founded in 1948, is a shining example. The peculiar and continuing

conditions in Hong Kong provided challenges that have been enthusiastically met by several bus makers, AEC, Daimler and Guy having become experts in supplying chassis suitable for carrying double-decked bodywork with seats for 100 or more. At another extreme are the high ground clearance lorry-based buses developed for rural African conditions by Albion, AEC, and Guy.

Inevitably in any activity so vital to a nation's interests as transport the vagaries of politics are hard to evade. For many years its involvement with production in Israel excluded Leyland from visible trading with Arab nations, while the famous dispute with America over the supply of Leyland buses to Cuba caught the public imagination and held it – something rare indeed in commercial vehicle matters. More recently differences with the countries of southern Africa have eroded once-loyal markets, together with those of Argentina and neighbouring states.

Top: Austin was never seriously in the bus building business, although occasionally a passenger version might be offered in the catalogues, almost as an afterthought. But selling to the passenger carrying market is quite different to the lorry trade and no doubt Austin felt efforts to market buses would not be justified. It followed, therefore, that such buses as were built on Austin chassis resulted from operators who had some objection to the usual lightweights, or who could get nothing else. Overseas, financing arrangements would no doubt affect decisions too. This 1951 export went to Lagos, Nigeria, and it seated 32. Mulliner built the body.

Above: The only 'BMC' now active in vehicle manufacturing is BMC Sanayi ve Ticaret, in Turkey, an operation in which a small shareholding is owned by Land Rover-Leyland. Sanayi took the larger bonneted BMC lorry models of the 1960s and adapted them for local manufacture, using BMC-origin diesel engines. The cab was designed for simple manufacture and repair, with flat sheet metal work and flat glass, and shows what can be done in producing an acceptable appearance without high-cost tooling. The Leyland name is displayed prominently on the Turkish products and so is Austin – or, in the case of this heavy version, Morris.

Revival

When an enterprise is in the kind of plight in which the British Leyland Motor Corporation found itself as the 1970s wore on the number of choices open to it gradually dwindles. Finally they are reduced to two: survive or die. So closely by then had the British government involved and identified itself with the affairs of Leyland that politically it was inconceivable that the company might be allowed to close its doors. And it was almost as unthinkable in the economic climate of the times that the organisation, by now the only British-owned motor vehicle manufacturer of any size, would be allowed to flounder on, making ever larger losses which could be underwritten only by the State.

In attempting to solve this unpleasant dilemma, the government, with a courage born of desperation, took the only feasible course open to it. Company management was reinforced, and large but finite quantities of financial aid promised – which would be delivered as and when the company revived. How the revival was to be staged was a matter for the company itself.

Earlier plans had in large part been based on the premise that greater integration of the many activities within the Corporation would help produce operating economies and make it easier to administer the whole, with an overall gain in corporate efficiency. Whatever the object the reality was very different, and one of the first acts of the new order was to separate the various parts of the whole into governable entities, within each of which failures and successes could be identified rapidly. Outward evidence of the change lay in a terse statement that since the name 'Leyland', after years of projection as a corporate identity, still meant heavy vehicles to most people it would henceforth be applied only to trucks and buses, not to cars. To thoughtful onlookers there was significance also in the now overly grand 'British Leyland Motor Corporation' becoming an wholly owned subsidiary of an almost self-effacing 'BL Ltd'. More tangibly, inward signs centred on a heartening and heavy investment in new plant and equipment, not to mention what amounted to a revival of vehicle design and development.

Moreover, for the first time in years the heavy vehicle division was getting its fair share of investment money. At the time that the Leyland Motor Corporation and the British Motor Corporation merged no one questioned the general opinion that the heavy vehicle side was strong and profitable, or that the volume car business was in a bad way and likely to get worse. It was therefore understandable that much of the available time and money was put into the car orientated activities – with, as it turned out, small effect. While the many ranges of products marketed by Truck and Bus remained young and generally acceptable, and markets were buoyant, this neglect appeared to be doing little harm: although in truth most competitors were quietly forging ahead in vehicle design, manufacture, and sales. Therefore the oil-induced economic crises of the 1970s caught Truck and Bus with ageing product lines, falling sales, and no available cash with which to combat either.

In its way Marathon was a melancholy illustration of what was happening within the division. Early in the decade, faced with an ever-growing influx of continental models tailored for the 32-40 tons premium tractor market, and possessing nothing of its own with which to defend itself, Leyland put together satisfactory combinations of existing components and proved in gruelling demonstrations that the results could equal much of the opposition. But the shortage of funds meant

Within a remarkably short space of time coach operators in Britain turned from being home-product only users into buyers of imported vehicles. Many of these are of high specification and advanced design, so in addition to its Tiger chassis, which compete for what may be termed conventional markets, Leyland Bus produced the Royal Tiger, usually with Doyen bodywork by group member Roe. The Royal Tiger is a spaceframe integral, with strength overall depending upon the body framing. There is, however, a floor frame which carries and locates the running units, but it is not strong enough without reinforcement to be driven. The engine is rear-mounted, allowing ample luggage space under the floor, and the Doyen body has one-piece panels and bonded windows.

Once the new Leyland assembly plant had got underway with the Roadtrain members of its T45 family, others followed in quick succession. Replacing the medley of middleweight rigids came the Freighter range (**top left**) – eleven load carriers for operation at gross weights from 11 to 16 tons. Freighter is essentially a descendant of the old Clydesdale, but with a choice of engine and transmission options which are able to match it to applications that can reach from small tipper work to large haulage operation, including the increasingly significant inter-urban distribution. Providing a downward extension to the Roadtrain artic tractors is now the Cruiser (**top right**), a light-weight unit designed for running at between 32·5 and 35 tonnes. Like the rest of the T45 vehicles it is built up from a combination of components developed from units used in earlier products, and also some bought in from specialist makers. The C40 cab, in day or sleeper form, is used throughout the range.

Above left: After years when the group had no effective answer to increasing competition in the light commercial vehicle field, Freight Rover bounced back with a revision of the old-established Sherpa which began to sell well – and also this new wide body version. It takes the Sherpa range up to the significant 3·5 tonnes gross weight limit; within the basic three-model range the Freight Rover can offer factory-built panel and Luton vans, high roofs, dropside bodies, chassis-cabs and an 18-seater minibus. A four-wheel-drive version and a caravan are also included in the catalogue. Unladen weight has been kept to a minimum, and the company says that aerodynamically the big Sherpas are superior to most cars.

that no new cab could be provided – and by this time cabs had become second only to operational reliability in the list of buyers priorities. Instead the old established Ergomatic cab was dusted down, retrimmed, and perched high on the new tractor chassis – just when the continentals were putting the finishing touches to new highly fashionable low line cabs.

Production was slow to get under way, and early unreliability was not combated quickly or effectively enough to prevent a poor reputation growing – and in any case Marathon was soon outclassed by a whole new army of imports. And in the muddled fashion that had by then become a hallmark of BLMC as a whole, some Marathons were made at the old Guy plant in Wolverhampton and most at AEC in London. The last, incidentally, were produced by Scammell, that well-known group orphanage at Watford.

Marathon was one product from three factories, not counting those of the component suppliers, and this in turn illustrated another problem area: too many plants, and only one of them fit for comparison with those elsewhere in Europe. The Albion factory in Glasgow was still producing what were recognisably Albions; Bristol in the West Country still made Bristols; Guy at Wolverhampton built Guys; and Daimler in Coventry built Daimlers. Scammell, to the north of London, made Scammells, and AEC in west London made AECs. In Bathgate modified but still recognisably BMC commercial vehicles were being built. Nearly all

these separate factories made products which overlapped and competed with each other: Leyland itself competed with all of them.

The one bright star in the catalogue was the Workington factory, set up and heavily tooled to produce what amounted to the most advanced single decked bus in the world. Of the National it can fairly be said that the superiority embraced passenger comfort, serviceability, and manufacture, even if all three were achieved only after an initial settling period which became unduly prolonged due to lack of funds. But National was, like its parents, a creature of government. Originally conceived and encouraged by an officially induced assumption that Britain as a whole was about to forsake its century-old allegiance to double decker buses, rapid political changes of mind re-established double deck operation as firmly as ever. As a result the Workington plant has rarely approached its theoretical production capacity. It is instructive too to recall that for some years after Workington began delivering its fully integral ready-to-run Nationals, Park Royal, Roe, and Eastern Coach Works were all in business bodying separate chassis produced elsewhere.

In the circumstances it seems perverse to regard the catastrophic collapse in demand worldwide for all kinds of vehicles, which ushered in the 1980s, as any better than yet another disaster added to the many already assailing a crumbling Leyland. Yet in almost every regard except that of finance the slump happened at a

Above: Unlike most of its contemporaries, the Marina range of cars and light vans was styled as an entity, with the satisfactory result that the commercial versions looked as much an integrated design as the cars did. Both van and pick-up versions enjoyed steady if unspectacular sales, suffering many of the woes which afflicted the BL car division. With the general upturn in group fortunes these light commercials benefited from improved quality control and therefore acceptance. Although, like the Metro and Sherpa, they are not products of Leyland Vehicles, they are generally regarded as downward extensions of the commercial vehicle range.

Right: Broadly, it could be said that the Olympian was intended to provide a less expensive alternative to the Titan, while at the same time providing a logical successor to a long line of Bristol-built double deckers, as well as a chassis for others to body. In the event it has become the standard Leyland Vehicles offering for at least the 1980s and possibly longer: both Titan and the Bristol works have succumbed to economic pressures; Olympian is now built at Workington. Eastern Coach Works, the long-time partner of Bristol, has bodied the chassis and so has Roe: this Olympian, in service with National Bus subsidiary Devon General, was the last to be produced by the Bristol plant.

The Roadtrain range of premium tractors, it was generally admitted, proved to be well thought out and introduced in impeccable fashion. Both aspects were more important than usual, since Roadtrain carried the great and unusual burden of re-establishing the company among the world's leading makers of heavy vehicles. The new tractors, introduced in 1979, are built to haul gross loads from 36 to 40 tonnes, and incorporate several major proprietary units, including engines and gearboxes. The low-profile C40 cab system, on which a vast amount of time and money was spent on development, is used throughout the present range of vehicles. In the event Roadtrain proved to be a success, and it became a secure foundation for other new products.

Even during the baddest of the bad days the Unipart operation, supplying a huge range of car spares and accessories, not only for group products but also cars made by rivals, earned a steady living, and prospered. Inevitably the commercial vehicle business was explored to see if a similar operation could be created there. It could, and Multipart is the outcome. There are very few heavy vehicles which do not contain some of the 150,000 or so all-makes components carried by Multipart, which also has the backing of a factory devoted to producing replacement parts for obsolete vehicles built by the group and its forebears.

Top right: Towards the end of its production life the Terrier unexpectedly blossomed forth as a chassis suitable for experimental work. It is inherently a lightweight and fuel-efficient design, and in a renewal of interest in battery-electric propulsion during the late 1970s Leyland collaborated with W & E, which normally produces battery-powered milk floats, in producing a normal-sized but electric Terrier. The vehicle meets the criteria usually laid down for such vehicles in that it is 'traffic compatable', able to keep station in busy urban streets and to provide a useful mileage between charges. High initial price should be susceptible to volume production.

Above: For many years BLMC depended on two old established, and once rival products to maintain its presence in the coach chassis market. When finally it was possible to replace the ex-AEC Reliance and the ex-Leyland Leopard another of the old animal names, Tiger, was chosen for a heavyweight under-floor-engined chassis which brought together an assembly of features which make it one of the best of its kind. In common with other products in the present Leyland Vehicles range, a wide range of specification options are available, particularly in the transmission, to meet operators' requirements. Air suspension is standard, and few builders would have difficulty in bodying the flat-topped chassis frame.

In keeping with its long traditions of vehicle supply to countries in what is known as the 'Third World', Leyland Vehicles has two model ranges specifically intended for places where the going is tough and operating conditions less than perfect. Smaller of the two is Landmaster (**right**), built up in large part from components used in chassis made at Bathgate, but with a bonnet to make engine access easier when workshops are ill-equipped or non-existent. Landtrain (**opposite**) is a much larger proposition, and it can operate at up to 65 tonnes gross combination weight. This fleet of Landtrain six by four tippers, carrying 16 cu m-capacity bodies for civil engineering work, were part of a large consignment sent to the Falkland Islands, but both Landtrain and its smaller brother also sell throughout the Middle East, Far East, and Africa.

While the rest of Leyland Vehicles was fully engaged in producing designs worthy of the company and suitable for the late 20th century, Scammell busied itself with two basic models that were thoroughly in keeping with its past. For military and similar use came the Commander (**centre**), a double-drive, six-wheeled tractor capable of transporting unit loads of up to 65 tons weight. More generally applicable is the S24 range of bonneted chassis (**below**), made as six by four or six by six wheels driven. As load carriers they can gross at from 30 to 44 tonnes, and as tractors up to 150 tonnes. Since they are built up from proprietary components a huge range of specifications are possible.

singularly fortunate time, for it made possible all kinds of harsh decisions and actions throughout BL as a whole that would have been much more difficult if the prime preoccupation of the company had lain instead with satisfying an insatiable market. Throughout industry, in the climate of the early 1980s plant closures and wholesale changes in work practices became almost expected. British Leyland had no choice but to fully engage in both, and within a remarkably short space of time Leyland Vehicles turned, in fact as well as aspiration, into a single homogen-

eous business. That was a sizeable achievement in itself, but perhaps even greater were the technical successes reached by the product and production engineers.

The former, at any rate, had had something of a headstart, for back in the darkest days of BLMC the group had committed itself to a new range of heavy trucks and began fundamental research work. This project was given the greatest priority by BL and work forged ahead at a much accelerated pace. Meanwhile the clearly laid out financial plan with which the company was now armed made possible a complete reassessment of commercial vehicle production facilities, with the almost inevitable conclusion that there were far too many factories assembling too few vehicles, too many factories producing parts of vehicles, and that the buildings and equipment of both were in large part obsolete. It inevitably followed that one large new plant containing the most modern equipment could produce a unified range of chassis that would replace all the existing products, and that far fewer components production facilities were needed. Moreover, in future the company would make fewer of the parts it needed and would instead buy in from outside suppliers.

Expressed in such terms the overall policy was hard to oppose, despite much local dismay. The National bus plant had been placed in Workington as a deliberate contribution to the economy of an industrially depressed region and there was therefore some hope that perhaps the new truck plant would in similar manner become a prize worth having. It soon became evident, however, that an area as deserving as any was the Leyland

homeland in the north west. Not only would abandonment there of vehicle manufacture add substantially to already worsening local economic problems, but within property already part of the old Leyland Motors estate lay a 'green field' site that was in almost every way ideal for the projected assembly hall. Again, once the decision was made work proceeded at an unprecedented rate and within two years heavy tractors in the T45 Roadtrain range were rolling off assembly lines which probably had no equal in the world. Indeed so great was the newfound sense of urgency within the company that the factory itself was still far from complete when vehicle production began, but rapidly both the plant and the range of models it produces were finalised and settled down, the latter to begin winning back a little of the market share that once would have been its own as of right.

During these momentous times, for what is now known as Leyland Trucks, activities within the company were not standing still on the bus side of things. The revival of home market interest in double deckers had already led to a great deal of research and development work being invested in a single replacement for both Atlantean and Fleetline, and the first Titans were delivered by Park Royal during the last months of the old regime. Titan, an integral design, was deemed by many potential buyers to be too complicated and expensive for their needs and a version with a separate chassis went into production at Bristol. Apart from the National, Leyland was still producing a heavyweight single-decked chassis, the Leopard, and the last of these were made alongside T45 trucks, while an existing factory building on the same site

was refurbished for Leyland Bus, and tooled up to produce a new premium quality chassis, the Tiger and its relations. More adventurous still, not far away at Chorley, another separate enterprise, Leyland Parts, was establishing a full-scale production plant devoted to making components needed to service the many obsolete makes and models still in use around the world, and to organising Multipart, which markets replacement items not only to owners of Leyland-origin vehicles, but to users of rival makes as well.

For the smallest commercial vehicles sold by the BL companies responsibility still lay with the Midlands-based car division, but in another move designed to give distinct activities their own identities the Sherpa range of panel vans and derivatives was separated out as Freight Rover, part of Land Rover UK Ltd. Ital, Mini, and Metro vans stayed with Austin Rover, which title embraces the BL volume car business. From almost every point of view that is the logical place for them to be, and with their exception and in what appears to be the most enduring reshuffle of company names and responsibilities the Land Rover-Leyland Group was given the task of overseeing all the commercial vehicle interests of BL throughout the world. Aveling Barford remained a separate entity.

This unprecedented and fundamental reconstruction of the operation was brought largely to completion against a trading background which worsened as the weeks went by. In its first five years of existence BL saw the home market for all kinds of commercials halve, and exporters were in no better plight. Profound changes within the company were an intrinsic part of the survival

Right: Apart from the Constructor models, which are an integral part of the Leyland range as a whole, the Scammell factory is used to producing low volume and special chassis of all kinds. The S26 range comprises four, six, and eight-wheeled units for heavy duty work, fitted out for load carrying, and as articulated or ballasted tractors. All of these use more or less standard Leyland cabs, and Constructors carry 'Leyland' just under their windscreens – with 'Scammell' in rather smaller lettering further down. For unlike every other Leyland Vehicles constituent the Scammell name is deemed sufficiently valuable commercially for it to survive: the S26 range, as this early picture shows, nearly used it in full.

Below: In the revival of BL fortunes the Mini Metro car assumed a psychological importance out of all proportion to its true significance. It is no more than one member of a range of new products, but because it became the first to emerge every aspect of Metro – not least its sales figures – generated anxious public debate. In the circumstances the publicity alone would probably have caused it to succeed, but fortunately it proved also to be a sound vehicle and good value for money. Many early Metros were put to work in light delivery, but soon the company offered a proper van version.

A mutually profitable partnership over many years was the liason between Leyland, DAB of Denmark, and the Swiss Saurer. DAB is a long-standing subsidary of Leyland which in addition to building bus bodywork graduated to producing integral vehicles, many of which used Leyland components. Then in the early 1970s the Danes and Swiss began a collaboration which resulted in a range of single-decked buses (**right**) in which the running gear could be of Saurer or Leyland manufacturer, or both. The articulated unit (**opposite centre left**), another joint product of the three, was imported into Britain for demonstration purposes during a shortlived interest in the type. Among other people who showed interest in it was London Transport, which invited it to manoeuvre among parked ranks of Routemasters and AEC Regents.

The Workington plant, producing National single deckers, had in large part resulted from an industry-wide and government-supported supposition that the double-decked bus had had its day. This proved not to be the case, and Workington as a result was never fully employed. Yet, like other modern production facilities in the company, it is among the best of its kind in the world; this is the fully-equipped vehicle preparation and test centre (**opposite bottom**). Workington also made it possible for the newly reinvigorated Leyland Vehicles to demonstrate its determination to put its business on a sound footing. When Park Royal, after building a few dozen Titans (including these first three, **right**), demonstrated its unwillingness to alter work practices to something more in keeping with the changed climate, along with Eastern Coach Works, there was ample space waiting at the National factory to take in the double decker.

Left: One of the oddest aspects in the British Leyland story was and is the apparently charmed life led by Scammell Motors, and this plant still keeps a distinct identity – although now within Leyland Vehicles after some years as a member of Special Products. There is logic in both groupings, for many Scammell-built chassis are destined for the construction industry and so are at home among the road rollers and graders of Special Products. On the other hand, some are equally suitable for ordinary haulage. Among its staple products now are the eight-wheeled Constructors, equally suitable for tanker as for tipper work: there is a six-wheeled version too.

Above: Much of the inexpensive development work on the present range of lorry chassis had been carried out during the years when Truck and Bus was starved for investment money, and so when finally Leyland Vehicles received authorisation it had something of a flying start. Inherent in plans for new products was a new plant in which to make them, and on a site within the Leyland factory estate there quickly arose what was probably the best-equipped factory of its kind – certainly in Europe, perhaps the world. After assembly all vehicles are prepared for use without leaving the assembly hall, and they all have to meet strict performance criteria in this rolling road test bay.

plan, but extreme economic pressures made it all but impossible to soften the impact on individual plants. The AEC-Park Royal factories were once seen as the focal point for bus and coach opera-tions, but neither, it became clear, was necessary or could be afforded. AEC closed almost without trace, and Titan moved to Workington, where ample space awaited its arrival. Great efforts were made to restore prosperity to Guy, and for a while it seemed the factory could make its way by concentrating on vehicles and assembly kits destined largely for third world countries. The collapse of those economies also put an end to Guy. Bristol had become virtually a one-model factory, and again the much more modern Workington plant had more than enough space to accommodate the Bristol output. Albion was in a better position in that for many years, in addition to assembling its own chassis, it had acted as a main supplier of drive axles and gear boxes to the rest of the group. When chassis work finally ceased component production was modernised and expanded to fill the vacant space. Bathgate too survives, assembling chassis and producing engines.

But the most extraordinary component of the modern Leyland Vehicles is Scammell which, on the face of things, should have been as vulnerable to dismembering and extinction as any of the others that have gone. Yet despite being a long way from the present focus of commercial vehicle activity it not only builds still the great special purpose vehicles with which its name is synony-mous, but also produces the six and eight-wheeled Constructors, models which are an integral part of the present Leyland range of on-road chassis. What is more, the Constructor cab badge even includes the Scammell name, all of which seems to indicate that sentiment is not yet quite dead within the group.

Something other than sentiment, no doubt, has led to the choice of trading names now used by Land Rover-Leyland companies abroad, for despite many adversities the company main-tains a strong and growing presence in many places. There are Leyland Albion companies in East Africa, Uganda, and Tanzania, and Leyland Motors in both Zambia and Ghana. The Leyland Motor Corporation lives on in East Africa and Malawi, and BMC still operates in Turkey. There is even an Austin Motor Company on the register, but it is currently dormant. Most of these, and some others, are ultimately owned wholly or largely by Land Rover-Leyland International Holdings, but the wish of many countries to have a say in their vehicle supply industries means that in some operations ownership is shared with local interests – indeed, in the case of the Turkish company BMC Sanayi Ve Ticaret, that sole re-mainder of an earlier time, the LR-L share is less than five per cent. More typically, though, is the Indian Ashok Leyland, where about half the shares are held.

The activities undertaken by these overseas associates vary widely. Ashok Leyland manu-factures a range of vehicles and engines; in Denmark Leyland DAB makes buses only; some of the African concerns are sales outlets, while others assemble vehicles from kits of parts. In South Africa and Nigeria factories not only assemble BL group products but also those of other makers, under contract. Perhaps, though, the most useful indicator of where the immediate future lies are the two wholly owned European subsidiaries, Leyland Vehicules Industriels and Deutsche Leyland: for if Leyland, in any of its guises, is to survive, it must perforce become a European power.

Index